*Can Anything Good
Come Out Of
Bawcomville?*

Joel Hemphill

Can Anything Good Come Out Of Bawcomville?

Trumpet Call Books
P.O. Box 656
Joelton, TN 37080

www.thehemphills.com
www.trumpetcallbooks.com

Can Anything Good Come Out Of Bawcomville?
ISBN: 978-0-9825196-4-6

Copyright © 2012 by LaBreeska Rogers Hemphill

All rights reserved.
No portion of this book may be reproduced in any form
without the written permission of the publisher.

Printed in the United States of America

Unless otherwise indicated, all Scripture taken from
The Holy Bible: King James Version.

Acknowledgments

~~~~~~~~~

First, I am grateful to my husband Joel who allowed me the privilege to write about his interesting life as a boy, and to recount the stories that he told me from the time we met. Then as I wrote, he meticulously went back over each chapter to make sure it was the way he remembered. Thank you Darling! It was a great journey into the past!

To Dawn, our secretary. Every word had to pass through the keys of her computer, over and over again. Yet, she did it with interest and enthusiasm. Dawn you are the greatest!!

To Joy McKenzie, our editor. *"Thank you"* doesn't seem adequate to have such an awesome and talented lady to help Joel and me in our diverse writings. Joy you are a blessing to us from the Lord and we love you!!

A very special *thanks* to Lynsae Harkins of *Lynsae Design* for the cover artwork and to Nancy Carter of *Quality DigiPress* for the interior layout and design. Girls you are the best!

A big *"thank you"* to Joel's sisters Anna Gayle, Rita, Brenda, Juanita, and others for adding their memories that helped to confirm and enrich Joel's story.

I am also grateful to our dear friend Kenny Chilton for allowing us to add his miraculous testimony for the glory of God. I am sure that it will inspire many and bring hope to the hopeless!

A big *thank you* to all the colorful characters that passed through Joel's life in those crucial years of growing up. He learned valuable lessons from so many individuals by whom he was loved, corrected, inspired, and led into paths of righteousness. Because of this Joel humbly says, *"I am a debtor."*

Table of Contents

Foreword		11
Chapter 1	The Flood	15
Chapter 2	Bawcomville	29
Chapter 3	Sister Bea	41
Chapter 4	Close Calls	51
Chapter 5	Best Friends	57
Chapter 6	Pastor W.T. Hemphill	77
Chapter 7	Great-Grandfather Tilman	113
Chapter 8	Lenwil School	127
Chapter 9	Taking Communion	139
Chapter 10	Hunting	147
Chapter 11	They Saw It On The Radio	155
Chapter 12	The 38 Special	163
Chapter 13	The Church	175
Chapter 14	Poor Little Robin	191
Chapter 15	Christmas in Bawcomville	201
Chapter 16	Old Burr Head	207
Chapter 17	Family Road Trips	213
Chapter 18	Joy Riding With Raymond	229
Chapter 19	The Big Tease	235
Chapter 20	West Monroe High	243
Chapter 21	The Louisiana Hayride	249
Chapter 22	The Gospel Singers from Indiana	255
Chapter 23	The Tent Meeting	265
Epilogue		271

Dedication

~~~~~~~~~~~

In Memory of

Pastor and Mrs. W.T. Hemphill

Forward

When Joel and I married we were both seventeen, he was only one month away from his eighteenth birthday. Our backgrounds were very different. The main thing that we had in common was our love for each other and the Lord and the desire to serve Him. My folks had traveled around all of my life, and by the time I was in the tenth grade, I had lived in eight different states and gone to eleven different schools. Joel, on the other hand, was settled in every way. I was awed by the life that he had enjoyed while coming up. Joel had the same friends, went to the same church, and could point out the many places that he had roamed all of his life. In those first years of our marriage, he laughed and told me about Raymond Heard, Jack Smith, and the good times with his dear friends, Garland and Alvin Jones, Alsey, Carl and Raymond Franks, and Ralph Beebe. From that time I have felt that the story of Joel's boyhood would be of interest to a lot of others as it was to me. But when I would mention it, he didn't think there was a story to tell.

I have written two books about my growing up and about mine and Joel's experiences as a couple, *"Partners In Emotion"* and *"My Daddy Played The Guitar,"* but decided several months ago to go ahead with this book. After writing the first few chapters and letting him read them, Joel understood my fascination with his up-bringing. He soon got the vision, and when I needed more information about his past, I would get him to reminisce as I wrote (in longhand) on legal pads.

Can Anything Good Come Out of Bawcomville has been a joyous adventure for the both of us. If I were to describe its contents I would say that it's a capsule of an era that is long past, filled with action, human nature, laughter, and inspiration. Joel's life was honest and simple, yet rich with people, adventure, and the business of living.

This is a true story, though a few names have been changed for privacy. It is a connected series of happenings during the first eighteen years in the life of a boy who lived and found love in a village in Northeast Louisiana. That boy is **Joel Hemphill**, and the village is **Bawcomville** !

Sincerely,

LaBreeska

Chapter One

The Flood

The Flood

*T*he swollen river left its banks and crept into Ouachita Parish like a predator on the prowl. Slowly and deliberately it came as if it had a mind of its own. No one had the power to stop the flood. It bullied its way into homes, businesses, schools and churches, swallowing up everything in its path. The low-lying areas of Ouachita Valley were its first victims as it put *Bawcomville* under water.

The year was 1945 and young Joel stood by in wide-eyed wonderment at all of the commotion that was going on around him. While everyone was rushing about, he was trying to obey orders and stay out of the way. His father was hurriedly cutting boards and nailing them to the inside walls of their house, making giant shelves then hoisting their furniture upon them.

Outside the water continued to rise. Their front yard already looked like a lake. All of Joel's senses were on alert, especially when he saw some of their neighbors rowing by in boats. What he was seeing and feeling spelled danger, but when he focused on his dad, he became more at ease. At five years old, Joel felt confident that his father had everything in control. But as capable as Brother W.T. Hemphill was as a pastor and leader of the community, he couldn't stop the flood. He tried everything within his power to ride it out, hoping that the water would soon crest. He had even built a wooden walkway from their front porch, some two and a half feet high and thirty yards long, in order to access another building that was a tiny two-room bungalow they called the "little house," also referred to (with a smile) as the "prophet's chamber." Dad had built it for the many preachers who came by needing a place to stay for a few days, and on occasion, even weeks. The "little house" stood a few feet higher than their main dwelling, and as the water continued to rise, the family began using it as an alternative. Then what they dreaded and tried so hard to avoid happened; their home was flooded! When Dad saw that the water was creeping inside and his efforts were futile, he loaded his family (along with their dog Lucy and a few belongings) into a boat, and headed for higher ground. It was three miles to the levee where he had parked the car, and he rowed all the way. Other families had also parked their vehicles there and were unloading from boats as well.

Forced from their homes, many misplaced families moved in with relatives. Others moved into the C.C. camp in West Monroe, a facility provided by the government. These *Citizen Conservation* camps were work-camps, setup all over the country by President Roosevelt on the same order as the W.P.A. *(Work Projects Administration)*. In later years, the camp in West Monroe became Kiroli, a nice park that still exists today. As for Joel's family, they moved about fifty miles to Winnsboro, Louisiana, where Dad Hemphill, along with his father, Tilman Beauregard, had established a church in 1920. That assembly was temporarily without a pastor, so they moved into the parsonage behind the church.

The Hemphill family was blessed to have a place to stay and was thankful for it. But being uprooted from their home and familiar way of life was a drastic change for everyone; it took some getting used to. Joel's mother suffered the most. She feared cooking on the old kerosene stove that was part of the parsonage furnishings - and was always afraid that it would blow up. Mom's anxiety over that old cook stove was a daily occurrence.

The Winnsboro church was delighted to have the Hemphills and helped in every way they could by sharing with them what they had. The Townsends, who were members of the church and longtime friends of the family, had a farm close by. Their smokehouse held sides of bacon, hams and link sausages, hanging from the rafters. Joel had never seen such abundance, and the smell of that smoked meat made a lasting impression on him. He and his older brother Daniel would go there a couple of times a week and bring back two gallons of skim milk for drinking and for Mom to cook with. Money was scarce but those farmers had plenty of home grown food and shared it with Preacher Hemphill and his family. They brought what were called "poundings" and dropped them off at the parsonage. It was usually rice (grown in abundance in Louisiana), fresh eggs, vegetables, canned goods (such as fig preserves and mayhaw jelly) and on occasion, a chicken or a piece of fresh beef or pork. Brother Hemphill also cut hair while there to help with their finances. He had been a barber as a young man and had his clippers with him, so the boys from the church and neighborhood came to him for their haircuts. Dad had a stool in the yard behind the parsonage for them to sit on, and those who didn't have the small amount in cash could bring a dozen eggs or a chicken, etc. with which to pay.

Living in Winnsboro was okay, but everyone was happy when the water receded and they could go home. In a matter of weeks, Joel's family was back in Bawcomville cleaning up mud and silt and once again enjoying their familiar routine.

Those scenes and experiences of the flood of '45 made an indelible imprint upon Joel's mind and became some of his first childhood memories. But his story begins elsewhere.

Can Anything Good Come Out Of Bawcomville?

Fresno California

Joel Wesley Hemphill was born on August 1, 1939 in Fresno, California, to William Tilman and Viola Beatrice Brown Hemphill.

Brother Hemphill, after his wife Etta died of cancer - leaving him with eight children, several of whom were still at home, married Beatrice Brown on June 5, 1938. He was 45; she was 20. Times were hard, but he had heard that there was plenty of work in California. Many people that Brother Hemphill had won to the Lord in years past had migrated there and were prospering financially. They urged him to come, pointing out that he could work on the produce farms to support his large family while trying to find new direction for his ministry.

They landed in Fresno where the weather was pleasant and warm year round, and the produce farms, vineyards, and cotton fields were in abundance. Dad and the older children soon found work, and many places opened up for him to preach; he eventually started a church there.

They picked cotton in the San Joaquin valley. The soil there was rich and fertile, nourished by the San Joaquin River, a natural stream of water that flows from the Sierra Nevada Mountains and spills into the Sacramento River. This produced some of the finest cotton that stood waist high with bountiful bolls of fluffy white.

The Hemphills were familiar with the cotton fields of Louisiana. They had done their share of stooping, bending, dragging a cotton sack, and picking until their fingers were sore. But the cotton in California was far superior. There was less stooping

The Flood

and bending because it grew tall, and with those large bolls you could fill your sack in much less time. However, anyone who has picked cotton can attest to the fact that it is extremely hard work. The sun is unrelenting. You get hot, sweaty, itchy, thirsty, and feel as though you'll never get to the end of the row, much less the next one.

Juanita, one of Joel's sisters was a teenager of thirteen at this time. Being musically gifted, Nita always seemed to have a song to fit any occasion, even in the cotton fields of San Joaquin valley. One day when she was tired and miserable, she decided to amuse herself with a song that she had heard and began singing it loudly with feeling:

I won't work for a living
I'll get along alright without!
Some folks may work hard all day
But I'm telling you
I'm not built that way!

Some people work for love
And call it all sunshine and gain
But if I can't have sunshine without any work
I guess I'll stay out in the rain!

When the song fell on the ears of Dad Hemphill who was also hot and weary, with many of his church members working alongside him, he rose up and gently scolded her, saying, *"Daughter, cut it out!"* Of course that's all it took to bring Nita's performance abruptly to an end.

Fresno was a great place to live for many reasons, including a diversity of citrus trees growing fruit in people's yards, but Dad wasn't happy there. Mom Hemphill recalled that when she and the children went to town or on outings on their days off, Dad stayed behind to pray. All through Mom's pregnancy with Joel, Dad Hemphill spent a big part of his time in prayer. He needed guidance. He was seeking God for direction for his ministry!

After Joel's birth, the family stayed in Fresno until 1943. When Dad announced to Beatrice and the rest of the family that he had received an answer from the Lord and was going back to Monroe to start a church, they were crestfallen. Joel's mom didn't want to leave California. She loved it there and was also working in the fields, making spending money of her own. She resisted as long as she could, but when she realized that his mind was made up, she agreed. Beatrice Hemphill was a supportive wife. She respected her husband's decision and was willing to do whatever he thought best. So they packed up all of their belongings and headed south once again for the Bayou State.

Northeast Louisiana, with all its natural beauty, including many lakes and bayous filled with moss adorned cypress trees, and the flatlands covered with majestic oaks and more moss, along with gigantic magnolia trees making it seem almost tropical, still could not compare with southern California. But Monroe was experiencing growth and coming on strong. Evidence of its meager beginnings had all but disappeared, and it had become a flourishing, bustling city with a promising future as well as an interesting past.

The History of Monroe
Monroe's history goes back to February of 1783 when it was founded by the Spanish as a tiny river settlement. It began when Jean Baptiste Filhiol, known to the Spanish as Don Juan Filhiol,

The Flood

was appointed by the governor of Louisiana as commandant of the *Poste de Washitas* (Ouachita). Filhiol, a Frenchman, had served under Spanish Don Bernardo de Galnez against the English in Florida and was residing in New Orleans at the time of this assignment. That same year he, along with a party of settlers and soldiers, made their way up the Mississippi, Red, and Black rivers to the Ouachita in a keel boat and settled on the present site of Monroe to establish his post and assume his position.

Monroe is twenty years older than the *Louisiana Purchase*, making it the second oldest town in Louisiana after New Orleans. Following the transfer of Louisiana from Spain to France, the United States purchased this territory from Napoleon Bonaparte in 1803 for a total cost of fifteen million dollars. New Orleans was strongly influenced by the French but they had little effect on Monroe, which was more influenced by the Spanish, since it was Louisiana's Spanish governor, Don Estevan Miro who appointed Filhoil and commissioned him to build this fort in the Ouachita Valley. There were one hundred and ten settlers with Filhoil, mostly hunters and traders, which needed protection from the native Indians. They chose to settle along the east side of the Ouachita River. There they hacked through dense wilderness to build their fort, and named it *Fort Miro* in honor of the governor.

The word *Ouachita* came from the Indian tribes that inhabited the area and means "clear sparkling water" or "silver water." Fort Miro began as a trading post, and the Ouachita River became a great highway of commerce and transportation for the Ouachita Valley. The first steamboat to come to the fort was a cumbersome river craft, *The James Monroe*. It caused such a commotion as it loudly puffed its way into view that the community eventually changed the name of the fort to Monroe.

Monroe was incorporated in 1820 and for the next century grew into a thriving cotton center as gigantic steamboats made their way up and down the river. However, the largest port sprang up across from the fort on the west side of the river at Trenton, known today as West Monroe. That port became the greatest means of transporting cotton from the Ouachita Valley to New Orleans and St. Louis. A cotton mill was built along the river close by and was still in operation when Joel was a boy. The delectable smell of the oil that was extracted from the cotton seed to be sold for cooking, wafted from the mill and filled the air. Joel still has pleasant memories of that wonderful aroma.

For the South, cotton was a large-scale enterprise, and no part of the plant was wasted. The pulp that was left from making the oil had high protein content and was ground into meal and sold for cow feed and fertilizer. The husks were also removed and sold for fodder. As a lad, Joel went to the mill on a regular basis with his dad to purchase feed for their milk cows. The sweet aroma from the cotton seed oil made their mouths water. Brother Hemphill would often remark that it made him want to take a baked sweet potato and dip it into the oil before he ate it. One day, he laughingly said that to some of the workers, and they confessed that they had often done this while eating their lunches.

The land of Ouachita parish was rich for growing food as well as cotton and was also a hunter's paradise. There were deer, wild turkey, and ducks in abundance. The lakes and bayous were teeming with bass, bream and crappy. Yet Monroe's greatest asset was to be found later beneath its surface. In the 1920's, geologists discovered a natural gas pocket that was to make Monroe, for a while, the natural gas capital of the world.

When the Hemphills came back from California, they found the twin cities of Monroe and West Monroe bustling with life. Carbon plants had sprung up all around, the largest being on the north side of Monroe in the Sterlington area. The manufacture of carbon black from natural gas was a large industry. Carbon black, a valuable ingredient in making ink, carbon paper, automobile tires and many other products, was being shipped by barge to New Orleans and from there, all over the globe.

World War II
Another thing that was helping the economy to grow in north Louisiana, and in fact most of the U.S. at that time, was the production of war materials associated with our country's involvement in World War II. Numerous ammunition plants were putting people to work, and it seemed that there were jobs for everyone, both men and women. The U.S. had been reluctant to enter the conflict but had no choice when Japan bombed Pearl Harbor in December of 1941.

Britain had entered the war a year earlier, realizing that Hitler and his Nazi regime, along with the other Axis powers, including Japan, were out to conquer the world. They were ruthlessly crushing everyone in their paths, mercilessly terrorizing the weak, and were determined to eliminate the Jewish race. Winston Churchill, Britain's prime minister, delivered a speech in Europe with a "call to arms" in June of 1940, with these words:

> *"The Battle of Britain is about to begin. Upon this battle depends the survival of Christian civilization...if we fail, then the whole world, **including the United States**...will sink into the abyss of a new dark age..."*

On September 10, 1940, after Buckingham Palace was bombed, the war became for Britain, a bloody fight for survival. In spite of Churchill's urging's, the U.S. held back, seeing it as in our best interest to take care of ourselves and stay out of "Europe's war."

However, that all changed in Hawaii on the island of Oahu on December 7, 1941, when the Japanese bombed Pearl Harbor. The next day our president, Franklin Roosevelt, signed the declaration of war and plunged us into the fight. *"Remember Pearl Harbor"* became the battle cry. That slogan was printed on license plates, bumper stickers, posters, and even people's clothes. It was a grim reminder of our terrible loss, and the citizens of the U.S. became eager to retaliate. And retaliate we did, until Japanese Emperor Hirohito was sorry that he had come to blows with the U.S. Admiral Yamamoto, who commanded the Japanese fleet that made the attack, is known to have said, *"I fear all we have done is to awaken a sleeping giant and fill him with a terrible resolve."*

As terrible as it is, "the business of war" was a lucrative one. The war created industry and industry created jobs. Jobs in turn created a booming economy. World War II helped to bring our nation out of the Great Depression with a high price in American lives and treasure. Monroe also benefitted financially from the war in that it provided work for everyone. (The Air Force had even opened an air base at Monroe's Selman Field).

The Biedenharns
The Biedenharns were a successful family who also contributed to Monroe's growing economy. In 1944, the year following the Hemphill's return, the Biedenharns celebrated their golden anniversary of bottling *Coca-Cola*. Mr. Joseph Biedenharn was the first to put *Coca-Cola* in bottles and helped the famous soft drink to become the favorite it is today. As it happened, Mr. Joe was serving Coke from the soda fountain in his retail confectionary store in Vicksburg, Mississippi, when he had the revolutionary idea to sell it in bottles. He took his idea to the right people, and they agreed to sell him the world-wide bottling rights because they thought it wouldn't be successful. This innovative idea made Mr. Biedenharn a very wealthy man, because when the *Coca-Cola* company saw his success and wanted to bottle it themselves, they had to pay him a royalty on each unit.

In the fifties when Joel was a young man working at *Monroe Bearing*, a parts supply house, Joe Jr. would come in on occasion for supplies. There he often talked about his favorite subject, his *kitchen*. He had a twenty-five thousand-dollar kitchen when an average family could purchase a nice brick home for ten thousand dollars. This was a marvel to Joel. These successful people, having moved to Ouachita Parish, had a huge *Coca-Cola* bottling plant on Walnut Street that offered jobs to many, and they were also instrumental in helping launch *Delta Airlines* in 1924, a small crop dusting company that became the huge passenger airline. With its headquarters in Monroe, *Delta* started its passenger service from Love Field in Dallas, Texas, flying to Jackson, Mississippi, via Shreveport and Monroe.

However the most important source of jobs in Ouachita Parish remained the paper and bag industry in West Monroe. The *Brown Paper Mill* was an outstanding industrial enterprise, and had an output of *Kraft* paper that was unrivaled in the nation. It contributed vastly to the income of the twin cities through its payrolls as well as the related jobs in the pulp wood industry.

With all of the progress going on in the Twin Cities, one would assume that Brother Hemphill would start his new church in one of those two towns, but that wasn't the case. He even passed up the Brownsville area near the paper mill. To Mom Hemphill's dismay, Dad announced that they were "going to Bawcomville." That's where he would establish a church, and that's where they would settle down. And so they did. Two years later is when the flood covered Bawcomville, came inside the Hemphill home, and disrupted their lives. But the flood did not alter the growth of Monroe and West Monroe.

There was prosperity in the Twin Cities when Brother W.T. Hemphill came to that area to settle his family and start a church, but Bawcomville was a different story.

Chapter Two

Bawcomville

Bawcomville

Bawcomville was a small undeveloped settlement that stretched along the Jonesboro Highway, about five miles south of West Monroe. This road takes you past the paper mill, over the levee and down into some of the lowest flatlands of the area. Land was cheap in Bawcomville when the Hemphills settled there because it was on the off side of the levee, unprotected from re-occurring high waters. Its villagers were some of the poorest of the poor, many with large families having eight to ten children. And in Joel's boyhood some of them dwelt in make-shift houses which were little more than sheds, and some lived in tents.

To fully grasp the character and nature of Bawcomville in its early years, one would need to know that is was named after Dick Bawcom who ran a shabby roadhouse there called *Dick's Place*. This was a full-blown honky-tonk that sat in the heart of the village along the main road. Women of ill repute and lots of undesirables gathered there at night for entertainment and to drink themselves into a stupor, and their blaring music and brawling could be heard until the wee hours of the morning. Joel hated the place, and when he was a small boy he daydreamed of burning it down. He had seen his first adult fight there one day when they drove past it on the way to a family outing at the creek, and it ruined the trip. Having never seen television or been to the movies, he was traumatized to see one man beating another in the face until he was a bloody pulp, then leaving him unconscious, lying on his back in the gravel. Joel had nightmares over that horrible scene for months afterward. It made one wonder if any good thing could ever come out of such a backward place as Bawcomville.

It would seem that Brother W.T. Hemphill would have had to have been called to go there to establish a church. Nothing else but the call of God would cause him to take his family and put down roots in such a place. Surely he had a desire to follow the example of Jesus our Savior who sent these words to John the Baptist who was in prison at the end of his ministry: *"...and the poor have the gospel preached to them"* (Matt. 11:5).

Dick's Place was one of several places of business in the village and was located between two combination grocery store - filling stations on either end of Bawcomville. The grocery stores were worthy business establishments that met the needs of the community.

Owens store was the first to come into view after one crossed over the levee near the paper mill, and it played a major role in Joel's growing up. From it came most of the food that graced their table, and he landed his first job there as a teenager. On the same side of the road, down about a mile was Jackson's store. Then directly across the highway from Jackson's store was the *Jesus Only Apostolic Church* that Brother Hemphill founded in 1944. Everything the Hemphill family did in those days was centered around this church.

The church wasn't far from the Hemphill's house, only a half mile or so, and just a good walking distance, especially for the children. It set facing Martin Street, a gravel road that, after it passed the church, went down about a fourth of a mile, made a sharp turn to the left and up a slight incline. The road then became Schanks Lane and passed in front of the Hemphill dwelling, went about two more blocks, and intersected Jones Road, made another sharp left, and crossed the railroad tracks onto Jonesboro highway again. Schanks Lane, which later was named W.T. Hemphill Drive, helped to create a semi-circle from the front of Jackson's store to the front of Owens store. The street got its name from the Jimmy Schanks family that lived across from the Hemphills and were also members of their church.

A network of side streets, which were just narrow dirt and gravel roads connected to Schanks Lane and Jones Road, passed the homes of several of Brother Hemphill's church members. The Joneses, the Howards, the Stranges, and the Wages, were some of those families, many of whom were large in number and had sons Joel's age.

Joel loved the church, and he loved the wonderful people who filled the pews night after night, and Sunday after Sunday. Most were people who had been on the road to nowhere, had come to church, found the Lord, allowed the Holy Spirit to clean up their lives, and became somebody on the road to somewhere.

The core of the Bawcomville assembly was made up of genuinely born-again Christians. They came needing the Lord and weren't ashamed to bow their knees to repent at an altar of prayer. Something about that era produced an honesty in folk that was both inspiring and refreshing. Those were the days before microwaves, instant pudding, and dry-eyed conversions. In the Bawcomville church you either *were* or you *weren't*. Grey areas didn't exist. Giving oneself over to foul language, cigarettes, booze, or promiscuity just wasn't acceptable behavior. To rid yourself of those things, you simply repented with tears of regret and prayed until you got victory over them.

The members of the Bawcomville church knew the meaning of *"praying through."* That expression was common language and common practice during Joel's childhood. Today that term is rare and is replaced with the more modern phrase, "make a decision for Christ." Making a decision to follow Jesus is a must, but our experience with God must go further than mental assent. *We* change our minds, but it takes *God* to change our hearts and our desires, and the only way for that to happen is through earnest prayer with *"...repentance toward God, and faith toward our Lord Jesus Christ" (Acts. 20:21)*.

Pastor W.T. Hemphill was well respected in the community, so when the residents came together to form a citizens committee to deal with issues such as the periodic flooding, they appointed him as chairman of the board as well as Bawcomville's unofficial mayor. After the flood in 1945, they formed a "levee committee" and began to press elected officials to appropriate the funds to construct what is called a "ring levee." That levee was to connect with the one at the paper mill, and be constructed in the shape of a giant horseshoe to encircle and protect Bawcomville. One important key to securing the levee was the fact that God had given Brother Hemphill favor with their powerful congressman, Otto Passman, a Jewish man who joined in to make it happen.

The citizens committee could also be described as a "grievance board" that met from time to time to deal with those who engaged in illegal or improper conduct. One of the most difficult and perplexing problems of Bawcomville was how to deal with *Dick's Place*. The board finally convinced the sheriff's department of Ouachita parish to designate a deputy to come out and patrol the area. The deputy drove a pick-up truck and began showing up at the rowdy honky-tonk. But before long he started hanging out there, even on his days off, and became part of the clientele. Eventually the sheriff's department had to let him go.

Another grievance that the committee had to deal with was the actions of an ex-Boy Scout leader. The man lived in Bawcomville but had a homemade house boat that he kept docked at *Cheniere Lake*, about five miles from the village. They found out that he was corrupting the youth by gathering up the young boys and taking them there to swim, with the main requirement being that they couldn't wear clothes. When Joel was invited to go along he saw some shocking behavior that he immediately relayed to his dad. When the committee was presented with this problem, it didn't take long for them to put a stop to these activities.

It was a happy day when Bawcomville's ring levee was completed, but it took years. Before it could become a reality, there was another flood, in 1948, when Joel was nine years old. This time he and Daniel rowed down the streets in their dad's boat, observing the damage. Their next-door neighbors, the Price family, lived just down the hill from the Hemphill house in the bend of the road. Joel remembers boating up to the windows of their house and seeing their furniture floating around in the cold dark water. It was a sickening sight that made him sad, but what made Joel even sadder was when the water came inside the church.

The Pony
Well into Joel's adolescence there were no stock laws in Ouachita parish. The cattle had open range, and some were turned out daily to graze wherever they could find pasture. It was a common sight to see cows come down the road headed home in the evenings, lowing as they made their way to their own place to be fed and milked.

Another common sight was a herd of wild horses that roamed the area. On occasion, Joel would hear their thundering hoofbeats and feel the ground vibrate before they came into view. Then about fifteen horses would appear in a stampede of glory with nostrils flaring and manes flowing. It was a magnificent spectacle that came by their house and disappeared in a cloud of dust like a desert mirage.

During the flood of '48, the horses came charging down Schanks's Lane, this time with a beautiful Palomino colt accompanying his mother. Joel had seen the pony once before and had dreams of catching and taming him. The horses rushed past the house and down to the bend of the road where the water had backed up and covered the street. At that point, without hesitation, the herd plunged in and starting swimming across.

But when the little colt jumped in, he caught his foot in some fence wire that was under water, and started thrashing about and struggling to free himself. When Joel saw what was happening, he thought "Now is my chance!" Quickly he ran to the boat which was tied beside the road at the edge of their yard, planning to paddle out and rescue the pony. It's a good thing that his dad was close by and saw what was happening and immediately stopped Joel from following through with his plans. Dad Hemphill knew that the wild horse would never let anyone get close. He would have drowned himself and anyone that tried to save him. Joel's hopes and plans were dashed when his dad intervened. He couldn't see the danger; he just knew that he'd missed his big chance to catch that pony. Thankfully the colt eventually freed himself and swam off to join the others. This ended Joel's dreams of owning that beautiful Palomino pony.

Israel Becomes A Nation
That same year on May 14, 1948, Israel declared itself a sovereign state based on the U.N. resolution that granted them that privilege. Our President Truman recognized them immediately which helped give them legitimacy.

Joel will never forget the excitement of that historical occasion. Dad loaded up the family and drove across town to the Joe White farm where they talked for hours on the subject and discussed Bible prophecy. Brother Joe was a deacon in Dad's church, and he and his wife Donie loved to talk over Scripture with their pastor and were eager to see what the Bible said about this great event. Expectancy of Jesus' soon return was at an all-time high and spirits were soaring.

The two families sat and talked all afternoon and into the night about how Israel becoming a nation was a major end-time sign. Dad told them he believed that we were within a generation of the time when Jesus would come back to sit on the throne of his father David in Jerusalem and reign for a thousand years. According to Scripture, Jesus is to rule the nations in righteousness with a rod of iron, preparing the earth for *"the great white throne judgement"* of **Almighty God** who comes **after** the thousand years is ended. *(See Rev. 20:7-12).*

> *"And I John saw the holy city, new Jerusalem, coming down from God out of heaven...and I **heard** a great voice out of heaven saying, Behold, the tabernacle of God is with men, and he will dwell with them, and they shall be his people, and **God** himself shall be with them, and be their God. And **God** shall wipe away all tears from their eyes; and there shall be no more death, neither sorrow, nor crying, neither shall there be any more pain..." (Rev. 21:2-4).*

~~~~~~~~~~~~~~~~~

Brother Hemphill was glad to find that northeast Louisiana had attracted a large Jewish population early on, and he became friends with many of them. Among these were wealthy businessmen who had the finest haberdasheries and dry goods stores in town. The *Silversteins*, the *Liebers, the Sol Snyder Family,* and *Sig Masser*, were just a few of those connected with thriving businesses. Mr. Masser and his family owned and operated, *The Palace*, an elite clothing store that sat on the main street in the heart of town. It was one of the most elegant places to shop for ladies apparel in north Louisiana. Joel's sister Juanita went to work there in the cosmetics department while still in her teens, even though she wore no makeup. In those days, superficial color on a woman's face was against the teachings of many Christians. Mr. Masser was heard to say as a compliment to lovely Juanita, "Few women are pretty enough to go without make up." Lois, another sister, also worked at *The Palace* at the same time in the hat department.

Those girls were always proud when their Dad came into town and dropped by to say hello. But they soon found out that he came in to visit with the Jewish Mr. Masser, as well as them, to talk about one of his favorite subjects, *Israel*. Joel's dad loved Israel so much that he had considered moving there with his family, including his mother, in the 1920's and would have done so if they could have afforded to financially. His love for Israel was known to all of his family and many associates, long before it became a nation.

Brother Hemphill was up in years when he and Mom, along with Joe and Donie White, finally had the chance to tour Israel with a group of ministers and friends. He was so moved when he stepped off the plane in Tel Aviv, that he got down on his knees and kissed the ground.

Dad loved Israel so much that he never accepted the label of "gentile" for himself. He had no proof, but he believed strongly that he was Hebrew. He prayed daily for *"the peace of Jerusalem and all of scattered Israel,"* always ending that prayer by quoting the prophet Isaiah, *"...though Abraham be ignorant of us, and Israel acknowledge us not; thou, O Lord, art our father, our redeemer..." (Isaiah 63:16).*

It is safe to say that for Brother W.T. Hemphill, the two most important places on this planet were Israel and Bawcomville. In that order!

Chapter Three

Sister Bea

Sister Bea

Beatrice Hemphill was a raven-haired beauty with just a hint of Choctaw Indian features from her ancestors. This was Joel's mother. She was a wise, self educated woman who added strength to her husband's ministry. Beatrice was also an avid reader who kept up with current events through the daily newspaper and who had political savvy.

This unique lady stepped into her role as a pastor's wife like a pro. She and her husband were a team who took their work for the Lord seriously. Not only were they the shepherds of a local church but were much involved in community efforts. Mom served as president of the P.T.A. at Bawcomville's *Lenwil* school for years, and helped Dad Hemphill run the polls at Jackson's store when it came time to vote.

The church family called Beatrice, "Sister Bea," and Dad called her "Trissy." She bore him five children, Joel being the oldest; then there were Anna Gayle, Rita, David and Brenda. She was devoted to her husband and children and was also a very caring and attentive church mother.

Sister Bea seemed to always be doing a balancing act between her family and the church family. Countless times she burned the beans she was cooking while on the phone with Sister Jones, Sister Abraugh, Donie White, or some other dear saint who needed encouragement. She loved, listened, advised, mentored, and dealt patiently with all those who came to her, young and old. Sister Bea was a true mother in every sense of the word, a remarkable lady whose easy manner set the mood for a peaceful existence in the home and in the church.

It was a marvel how Sister Bea took everything in stride. Housekeeping didn't rule her. Actually she was pretty lax in that department. She had a few standard rules - like the beds must be made and the dishes washed - but after that the children had few household chores. And then there was the milking. Dad always had a milk cow or two, and this chore was under his supervision. Each of the children, including Joel, took his or her turn on the milking stool at one time or another.

The Hemphill Home
The Hemphill home was a big, old sprawling house. There was nothing about it that said affluence. Rooms had been added, one by one, through the years with no basic plan, and the furnishings were nothing to boast of. But it was a real *home* with a family whose roots sank deep into the Louisiana gumbo soil. This huge, haphazard house sat on six acres of undeveloped land. There was a wooden swing on the front porch that was typical of the period. When you entered the house and passed through the living room, there was a long hall with bedrooms off to each side. The hallway led all the way to the back of the house and opened into a very spacious kitchen. An unusual thing that one noticed right away about this kitchen was that it had two refrigerators. These always held an abundance of food, causing one visitor to nickname it approvingly, "super kitchen."

To get from the kitchen to the back porch you took a right turn and went through a big sturdy, home-made door. However, it wasn't the door that caught your attention; it was what was on the other side. There, stacked along the wall, were cases of soft drinks from the *Nehi* Bottling Plant in Monroe; *R.C. Cola, Grape, Orange, Creme Soda*, etc. There was an old fashioned Coke cooler with a sliding top - the kind that was usually found in grocery stores - stocked with the soda pop and quarts of milk from Dad's Jersey cows. These drinks were so cold it would hurt your teeth because the ice man came around twice a week to supply the cooler with ice.

The Hemphill home was a busy place and filled with life. Church members were dropping by daily, sometimes with a homemade cake or pie, or fresh veggies from their gardens. Visiting ministers were coming and going on a regular basis for Mom to cook a meal, or to stay for the night. Then there were the children coming in from the cow lot with the buckets of fresh milk to strain and put away. It was enough to overload any housewife, yet Mom Hemphill seldom lost her cool. She seemed to sail through all the commotion with the greatest of ease. Even her children's occasional skirmishes, that often included a race to see which one could get the newspaper first, didn't ruffle her. But there was a limit to Mom's patience.

The straw that broke the camel's back was Dad's "dairy." With all that Mom had to do, which included washing clothes on a wringer-type washer, there were times when those endless buckets of milk overwhelmed her. To come in from the washhouse and find all those dirty milk bottles lined up on the kitchen sink was more than she could take, and it would set her off. Mama would start her warpath with "Preacher!" (When she'd had enough that's what she called Dad.) When Mom said "Preacher" her voice would rise, and the kids would slip out of sight. Even Dad made himself scarce and laid low until the storm passed. But Mom had a way of getting things out in the open, airing her grievances, then letting them go. Those stormy times were few and far between, but it made everyone try a little harder to help shoulder the load.

What was first and foremost to the whole family was going to church; getting ready and being there on time. Mom was very proficient in that department. Anything and everything could wait until after church. On nights when they were having service, Dad would often say; "Shug (which was short for Sugar), let's hurry! It's against my religion to be late!" Even in the hot summertime, Dad would dress for church in a white shirt and tie with his "Jesus Only" pin on it, along with suit and hat. Many times he would have to wait in the car (with no air-conditioning) while Mom did last minute preparations. He'd sit there twirling a small hand towel for a slight breeze, and then stop to mop his face with it. Then he'd holler at Mom, "Come on Trissy, I'm sweating down!"

Beatrice Brown Hemphill was a great lady in every sense of the word. She had a gift for seeing through to the heart of a matter and could usually distinguish truth from error and had no problem calling a spade a spade. Joel's mother was fair and compassionate and would give away anything she had. *Things* just weren't that important to her. Coming from humble beginnings, Mom could spot selfishness a mile away. She detested it and went to war on it, making sure that she and her children were givers, not takers. It was a lesson they learned well, and it produced a basic generosity in her off-spring that is inspiring to see.

Mom Hemphill's wisdom and insight into human nature was remarkable and came out in her many sayings. Sometimes to warn Joel against keeping bad company she would say, "Son whatever you want to do, good or bad, you can always find someone to do it with you." He also remembers her praying through the years, "Lord give us true, thankful hearts," but her saying, "God is great and greatly to be praised," influenced him most.

The Browns
Joel was ten years old when his Granny Brown passed away. Emma Bacon Brown, Sister Bea's mother, was a slight, unassuming lady and one-fourth Choctaw Indian. She was the only grandparent that Joel had the privilege to know. His maternal grandfather, Jimmy Wesley Brown, died (at the age of forty-six) before Joel was born. He was a hard working man, a builder by trade, and his death left Granny Brown a widow at an early age with five children to raise. She worked night and day, took in mountains of clothes for washing and ironing, and cleaned the nearby grammar school.

The Browns were gentle natured, affable folk, and Joel credits his mother's side of the family as touching his life with a great deal of positive influence. He loved to visit his grandmother and remembers her meager existence. She lived in West Monroe near the paper mill in an old city bus that had been converted for use as a dwelling. The old bus sat behind her son Steward's house. Granny Brown's youngest son Billy was still single at that time and lived with her.

Billy (Uncle Bill) was Joel's hero. He taught him things, including how to play the guitar. Jimmy Rodgers' song *"All Around The Water Tank,"* was Uncle Bill's favorite tune, and they played it over and over again. Uncle Bill also had the first motorcycle that Joel saw up close. It was a thrill when he would come riding out to Bawcomville on it. Joel didn't know it then, but it was so old that even in the forty's, that old bike was almost considered a *dinosaur*. In later years, Uncle Bill laughed and claimed that he had "pushed the thing more than he rode it!"

Billy Brown was an inspiration to Joel. His easy laughter and good natured humor was a bright spot in his life. Joel looked up to him and longed for the day that he could be as tall as his Uncle Bill who stood a *towering* five feet, four inches high!

~~~~~~~~~~

Joel's mother, like most of the Browns, was not a demonstrative person, but had had some very intimate experiences with the Lord that she drew from. At one point in her life, the palm of one of her hands broke out in a rash that would not go away. If she happened to put it in water, the pain was unbearable, and this problem became a heavy burden. Mom went about her daily chores wearing a glove and performed her duties as a homemaker with great difficulty. No one could determine what caused the rash, whether it was "nerves" or perhaps a virus. Some thought it possibly had to do with the chemicals from the paper mill. Whatever it was, several of their friends suffered from the same thing. One church member had such a severe case that she was hospitalized.

This problem with Mom's hand tormented her night and day, and she was prayed for many times. She kept it covered with a medicated salve, but nothing helped. She was forced to live with it. Then one day when Mom walked into the back yard, a Scripture verse surfaced in her mind that says: *"I will therefore that men pray everywhere,* ***lifting up holy hands****..." (I Tim. 2:8).* Mama started weeping. She looked up and said "Lord, how can I lift up ***holy hands*** with a hand that looks like mine?" When

Sister Bea

she said that, something happened, and from that moment on, it began to heal. In a short time, her hand was restored and the problem never occurred again!

This was the atmosphere that surrounded Joel during his growing years. He was born and raised in a devoted pastor's home. He belonged to a God-fearing family and went to a church where the services were uplifting and exciting. He had a mother who loved, honored, and stood by her husband as he preached his heart out in Bawcomville. And the results were phenomenal. Change was gradual, but it came and it produced a wonderful existence in the lives of hundreds of people, including many who did not attend their church.

The Bawcomville church was the happening place to be. It's where you saw your friends, and where the Holy Spirit revived your love for God and people and gave purpose to your life. Church was where the music was, singing and clapping your hands and enjoying those wonderful old songs such as *Victory In Jesus, Love Lifted Me, Joy Unspeakable, Living On The Hallelujah Side, When We All Get To Heaven, At The Cross, Living By Faith, Camping In Canaan,* etc.

It was a happy, down-to-earth existence. Most of Joel's boyhood friends lived close by, went to the same school, had the same beliefs and were constant companions. This closeness had it pluses and its minuses, but one thing is for sure: there was never a dull moment. Joel had a rich, full childhood, the kind that most children today could not even imagine.

Chapter Four

Close Calls

Close Calls

The Gas Heater

Since Monroe was the natural gas capital of the world, most every home was heated by it. In those early days, the heaters were primitive and had very few safety features.

As a small boy, Joel slept in a tiny side room adjacent to his parents. His bed was next to a window with a screen and a wooden shutter. As strange as it may seem, there was no glass in it. To have the window open, you just unlatched the shutter and swung it out. Then to close it you pulled it forward, and then latched the shutter from inside. It was crude and simple but characteristic of the early days of Bawcomville. Their house at that time was a work in progress.

One night an elderly minister, Brother Marvin Redd, was staying with the Hemphills and Dad asked him to adjust the heater that warmed his, Joel's and Daniel's rooms when he started to bed. With a limited knowledge of gas heaters, Brother Redd accidently turned it down until the flame went out, then quickly turned the gas back on, thinking that he had regulated the heat. It was a cold night, and Dad saw that the shutter was closed and latched before retiring to bed. When he got up around five o'clock the next morning for his usual time of prayer, he was startled to find that part of the house filled with gas. Rushing first to Joel's bedroom which was nearest, he found him near death, gasping for breath, and blue from the inhalation. Quickly Dad turned to open the shutter but mysteriously it was already standing open! Dad then rushed in to wake Daniel and Brother Redd out of their near-death slumber, then began opening windows and doors all through the house to get rid of the gas fumes and to let fresh air in. Dad was praying and praising the Lord every step of the way. He knew that it was by God's mercy that the three of them had escaped death. Thankfully they all recovered without lasting effects, and Dad always believed that the Lord had sent an angel that night to open the shutter and save the lives of his darling boys and dear friend.

Other Mishaps
There were other occasions that could have had a disastrous outcome, like the time Joel jumped from the roof of the barn with an umbrella.

This was back during the time that World War II was still making headlines, with pictures of paratroopers jumping from planes with their parachutes and floating to the ground. This fascinated Joel. It gave him the bright idea that he could do the same thing with an umbrella. He searched the house and found a big one, then climbed to the top of the barn, opened it up and jumped. But instead of drifting gently to the ground, the umbrella gave way, turned wrong side out, and he hit the ground with a jolting "thud." Thankfully no bones were broken; just the breath was knocked out of him, and he wore a few bruises as a reminder of his folly.

There were more dangerous incidents that included the time he lassoed a calf and wrapped the rope around himself to make sure it didn't get away. The calf became spooked and began to run, dragging him around the pasture, through weeds, briers, and over a pile of tin. Again he came through with only scratches, bruises, and more of an education in "hard knocks."

The Sack Swing

The sack swing was a poor boy's luxury and turned many a mundane day into daring excitement. This swing could easily be made from rope found in abundance at the paper mill dump. A rough old feed sack, stuffed with rags and more feed sacks, was tied at one end of the rope, and the other end was tied to a stout limb of a tree, the higher the better! Any family could afford one of these innovative swings, so they became quite popular. Thanks to Daniel and the older boys, the Hemphills had one of the best ones in their neighborhood.

Joel was in the second grade when he brought some of his school chums home to enjoy the thrill of flying through the air aboard the swing. His friends loved the daring excitement of riding as high as it would go, then yelling, "Tarzan the ape man!" Joel wasn't familiar with that saying. He had never been to the movies and had no earthly idea who Tarzan was. About all he knew other than school was church and politics. At that time Mack Avant was a local politician, and his name was mentioned often around the dinner table. When it came Joel's time to jump on the swing, thinking he was saying what his friends were saying, he hollered "Tarzan *Avant*!" Completely puzzled, his friends wanted to know who *Tarzan Avant* was! When they asked him, he sheepishly had to admit that he didn't know either.

David, Joel's youngest brother was a good natured, freckled faced lad who was loved by the Bawcomville church. David loved them in return and absolutely adored his dad. When he was very young, one night in youth service, he misquoted a verse of scripture. When someone said, "That's not in the Bible!" David retorted, "Well if it's not, my Dad will put it in there." David was full of life and was always figuring out ways to have fun. He loved to ride "Billy" the big, long-haired he-goat they had acquired, and that had come to think he owned the place. Billy was cantankerous and smelly, but David enjoyed riding him. Then he'd come into the house smelling just like Billy. Mama would shoo him out the door, and he'd go right back and do it all over again. David also loved to ride the sack swing. One day he made a daring leap onto the swing from the highest point of the big metal slide in the front yard. The swing rope was worn by then and had weakened. When David threw himself onto it, the force of his body broke the rope and everything went crashing to the ground, the swing and David with it. His head hit a large rock that protruded just above the surface of the ground, and on impact, his body went limp and lay there motionless. Horrified, one of the children ran screaming for Dad Hemphill. By the time he arrived on the scene, several minutes had passed and David was lifeless and pale, with no sign of a pulse. Immediately Brother Hemphill fell to his knees and started calling on the Lord in desperation. He and the family were crying, praying and calling on the name of Jesus with all of their hearts. Just when it looked as if he was gone, David moved, took in a big gulp of air, then began breathing again.

There was no doubt in anyone's mind that God had raised David from the dead that day through earnest prayer and tears. It was a great victory for Joel's family and a wonderful testimony of faith for David. He knew that God spared his life for a purpose, and he has gone on to become a minister of the gospel, a pastor and prophet. Today, many lives have been transformed and blessed as a result of David's ministry.

Chapter Five

Best Friends

Best Friends

"Sister Hemphill! Sister Hemphill! Help!" Mom was startled by the sudden outburst. The voice got louder and louder, and then trailed off. In a few seconds, here it came again. "Sister Hemphill! Sister Hemphill! Come catch me!" Then the voice faded away.

It was the spring of 1946. All the windows were raised and the doors were open. Mornings usually came to life with the sounds of roosters crowing, cattle lowing, birds chirping, or an occasional dog barking in the distance. If a breeze was stirring you might even catch the sweet scent of cape jasmine, honeysuckles or other wild flowers in bloom. But of course it wasn't all pleasant. There was the sweltering Louisiana heat, the smell of the cow lot or paper mill, and the ever-present flies and mosquitoes to contend with.

~~~~~~~~~~~~~~~~

On a day like the one just described, Raymond's yell for help broke the silence of the morning. His desperate cry was coming through Mom's bedroom window. She was standing in her slip, about to get dressed for the day, but when she heard him she understood what was taking place. Eight-year-old Raymond Heard was circling the front yard on his new bicycle and he couldn't stop it by himself. Someone had to catch him and help him down. She was in a dilemma and didn't know what to do. Finally Mom ran out in her slip, grabbed his bike and helped Raymond dismount. She was embarrassed by the whole ordeal and told him not to come on his bike again without a call from his mother, who had to get him started in the first place!

Raymond was one of Joel's best friends. He was a fun-loving kid who never seemed to grasp the concept that every action produces consequences. He couldn't understand that just because we are free to choose our actions, we are *not* free to choose the outcome of them. As Raymond grew older, this lack of understanding became more evident; but as a child, his care-free nature helped to turn many an ordinary day into adventure. He threw caution to the wind as he and Joel greatly enjoyed life. They were buddies, and where you saw one, you usually saw the other. Having a friend to do things with was great, but this friend could also be a challenge.

Once at Christmas time, Brother Hemphill had been painting and hanging paper for the man who owned *Welch's Bicycle Shop*. He agreed to let Dad trade his work for two new *Schwinn* bicycles, one for Daniel and one for Joel. And Brother Heard bought Raymond a new bike that same Christmas. But the two younger boys had the same problem: their bikes were too big for them.

The bar that distinguishes the boy's bike from the girl's ran from under the seat to the handle bars. At seven and eight, Joel and Raymond's legs were too short to straddle the bar to shove themselves off. When Raymond and Joel (who was even shorter) got started they couldn't sit on the seat and peddle. All they could do was stand up and "pump" leaning from side to side, but that didn't discourage either one from riding. The only problem was that it became a family affair. Someone had to start them off, and then wherever they went, someone else had to be ready to catch them.

Joel's bicycle had a basket on the front. Since Mom Hemphill didn't drive, she was glad when she was able to send Joel to the store for a few necessities, which began as soon as he learned to ride. Mom would start him off, then call Waymel at Owens store, give him her order, then tell him to be watching for Joel so he could catch him. Crossing the Jonesboro Road presented a small challenge, but there wasn't much traffic on their road in the mid-forties. If a car was coming, Joel would just ride around until the coast was clear, and then cross over. Once he got to the store, he would circle the gas pumps and yell for Waymel.

Time eventually took care of all the circling, as the boys continued to grow. Those bicycles became their first taste of independence. They had wheels and could go places and do things that they hadn't been able to do before. However some places were too far to ride their bicycles, such as the paper mill swimming pool.

The Swimming Pool
Summers in Louisiana are extremely hot and sultry. The many swamps and bayous create a humid kind of heat that causes one to look for relief. Men in construction and those who work in the outdoors have to pace themselves in the summertime. Some start working long before daylight and quit around 1:00 in the afternoon.

As a respite from the heat, Brown Paper Mill, just three miles up Jonesboro Road, had built a nice big swimming pool for its employees and their families. Even though Joel and Raymond had no relatives working there, the temptation to go to the pool was more than they could bear. Joel convinced his dad that mixed bathing (men and women) was mostly on certain days and only in the afternoons (not totally accurate), and Dad finally agreed to let him go if he could find a way to get there. With that Joel and Raymond were off for more fun and adventure.

Hitchhiking
The boys were so excited for the chance to go swimming that they would walk the three miles if they had to. In their minds, whatever it took to get there was worth it. But once they got to the highway they thought of a better plan. They would hitchhike, which was then an accepted way to travel for those who couldn't afford a car. It was a common sight to see someone on the side of the road with his thumb in the air, flagging a ride, and many of those with automobiles were gracious enough to stop and give them a lift. That day, Joel and Raymond had stuck out their thumbs to several cars passing by without any luck. There was an old city bus that came out from town ever so often and made a loop through Bawcomville before returning. But it cost a quarter to ride, which they didn't have. Raymond saw it coming and said, "Joel, you dare me to hitch a ride with the bus?" Joel didn't believe he'd do it and said, "Go ahead." So Raymond held out his thumb and the rickety old bus came to a screeching halt just past the boys, and the driver opened the door. When they ran up to the bus, Joel told him sheepishly that they didn't have any money. The driver looked them over and said, "Well boys, I've already stopped now, so you may as well get in." They were happy for the free ride, but that was the last time they flagged down the city bus.

The West Monroe paper industry used hundreds of employees; some worked at the mill making paper, and others worked at the bag or box plants. There were many benefits for those who were fortunate enough to land a job with the main employer, Brown

Paper Mill, Inc. It was steady work, it paid well, and then of course there was the swimming pool. To this day, Joel doesn't understand how he and Raymond got in on that benefit, but they became regulars. The facility was nice and modern. It had bath houses (one for the ladies and one for the men) to change clothes in. It also had a full-time life guard and the tallest diving board in the area. The city swimming pool had a ten-foot diving board, but the one at the mill pool was twelve feet high. There was also one much shorter for the children to use. The boys were glad for that, and as daring as Raymond was, he stayed clear of the high dive.

On a sad note, one day when Joel and Raymond weren't at the pool, some teenage boys began to badger a young girl and challenge her courage to jump from the high dive. They kept harassing and egging her on until she finally took the plunge from the twelve-foot diving board. When she went down, she never came up. The poor girl took the dare and lost her life. That event dampened everyone's enthusiasm for a while, but before long, it was business as usual. The pool shut down everyday around one o'clock, then reopened later in the evening. The boys went only in the mornings and played hard; and when they left, they were wrung out.

On the way home one day, again they failed to hitch a ride and were exhausted. Then they saw a young man coming toward them on a bicycle. Raymond said, "Hey Joe, I'm going to flag him." With that remark he stuck out his thumb and surprisingly, the fellow stopped, and agreed to give them a lift. Joel, being the smallest, hopped up on the handle bars and Raymond climbed on the back and rode on what *they* called the *"luggage carriet"* (carrier). The poor little guy peddling in the heat of the day became drenched in sweat as he took them all the way to Owens store. There they dismounted and walked the rest of the way home. After that memorable excursion, Joel found out that the young man was simple-minded and his heart was touched by the kindness he had shown them.

Several years later, right after we were married, Joel and I were riding along in West Monroe. It was dark when we passed a man walking down the road. Joel said, "I should have stopped and picked up that fellow." I was incredulous. "What do you mean?" I demanded. "Would you put my life in danger by picking up a strange man on the side of the road?"

This was in the fall of 1957, and by then, some drastic changes had taken place in America's social climate. Shocking tales were being publicized about hitchhikers becoming predators. It was making folk reluctant to stop and help anyone along the road. To pick up a hitch-hiker would be taking a chance on losing your car, your money, or even your life. I wasn't ready to take that chance. That's when Joel told me the story of the boy who had picked him and Raymond up and rode them three miles on his bicycle. Then he said, "That's the fellow!" When he told me that, I said, "You've got to turn around and go back, and pick him up and take him anywhere he wants to go!" When the young man climbed into the back seat, Joel asked him if he remembered the incident. He smiled real big and nodded his head in the affirmative and kept saying, "affright, affright." Then Joel said, "Well, I'm one of those boys - the one that rode the handle bars." It made us both very happy to give him a ride. We were grateful for the chance to return the favor for the young fellow, and it was a good deed that came back to him like *"bread on the water."*

Diphtheria

Diphtheria, an infectious disease caused by a bacterium and characterized by weakness, high fever, and the formation in the air passages of a membrane-like obstruction to breathing, became an epidemic in northeast Louisiana when Joel was about nine years old. Homes were quarantined in an effort to keep the contagious disease from spreading. However, Joel came down with it and was deathly sick for days. After he was out of school for two weeks, his teacher became concerned and came to see about him. When she saw how sick he was, she later cried and told some friends, "I don't know if Joel is going to make it." It wasn't looking good for him. He was running high fever, and he had lost control of his legs. If one happened to fall off the bed, someone had to put it back for him. Anna Gayle, his younger sister, was very attentive to him and was usually the one to do that.

One day Joel's mother became so distraught over his condition that she went across the street and asked Sister Schanks to come help her pray for her boy. There had already been lots of prayer for his recovery, but Joel remembers the day that he received his healing touch from the Lord. It happened when his mother and Sister Schanks got down beside his bed and cried and prayed in desperation. From that moment on, he started getting better, regaining his appetite and the strength in his legs! He recovered completely and never showed any lasting effects. He was on his way to recovery when the parish health nurse came to their home to check the family and took a swab of Joel's throat. She found evidence of the germ and warned his parents that he was coming down with diphtheria. They didn't tell her he was just recovering from it. But because she found the germ she quarantined the entire family. For the next nine days, none of the children could leave the house, not even to go to church. Joel's older sister Mary Evelyn, *(Pudd* was her nick-name), also came down with the disease and she wasn't so fortunate. The disease settled in her left arm, leaving it mostly paralyzed.

The paper mill swimming pool was quarantined that year also. It seems that after the death of the young girl on the diving board and the diphtheria epidemic, the pool lost its appeal for many people, including Joel and Raymond. Joel doesn't remember going there much after that. In a short time it closed down, but that swimming pool helped two young boys enjoy many a hot summer day and gave them a storehouse of happy memories to reflect on in the ensuing years.

The Alligator
When Joel and Raymond found how easy it was to thumb a ride to the swimming pool they began to expand their horizons. When school was out one warm summer day they decided to hitch a ride into the town of West Monroe to look for a job. Their church friends, the Franks boys, Carl and Alsey, lived in town on River Front and they both had jobs sacking groceries at *Gentry's Grocery.* Joel thought he and Raymond could do the same, but he hadn't taken into consideration that the Franks boys were a couple of years older than they were. After making the rounds to several stores, they soon found out that no one was interested in hiring ten and eleven year old boys from Bawcomville.

While looking about town, they found many things to attract their attention. They came upon an area under some shade trees with a few old benches where elderly men were gathered, chewing tobacco and swapping yarns as they whittled with their pocket knives. The boys were glad to find someone to talk to, so they stopped and hung out with them to listen to their stories. Close by was a small building that housed a barber shop. There was a mudhole near the shop where the barber kept his four-foot alligator. It was a real treat when they found they could get a close-up look at the gator and watch him eat as the owner fed him scraps. Of course there was no shortage of alligators in that area. Many times after the floods and high waters, people would find alligators in drainage ditches in their front yards, under their houses, in garages, and even crawling along the highways. The swamps and bayous of Louisiana have plenty of the interesting creatures. All one has to do is shine a spotlight in the bayou at night, and they see fiery red eyes blinking like scores of Christmas lights on the surface of the water.

As plenteous as gators were and are, Joel has never lost his fascination for them. He knew that they were dangerous, but at the same time, awe-inspiring. So many stories and fables are connected to gators. Joel had heard of them trying to capsize boats if a fisherman had his dog with him, and many who lived close to the bayous told stories of missing dogs. There were also stories handed down about small children and even adults, missing from families who lived near bayous, supposedly apprehended by gators. The state of Florida has documented over fifteen such occurrences since records have been kept.

The Louisiana alligators are capable of these actions. Their large rounded bodies, with thick limbs and broad heads, and very powerful jaws that hold an average of seventy-five teeth, are notorious for their bone-crushing bites. An adult gator can weigh as much as eight-hundred pounds and can grow up to fourteen feet. Half of the gator's body length is his great tail; not only used for swimming, but also as a weapon. They get around very quickly in water and can remain submerged for about an hour. In fact, you can be in a boat, fishing close to one, and never know it until he decides to surface.

It is understandable that Joel and Raymond were glad for the chance to see and inspect a gator up close. That barber shop alligator marks the beginning of a long and interesting relationship between Joel and those deadly predators.

True Grit
When Joel couldn't land a job in the grocery stores, he found an ad in a weekly paper called *The Grit*, a national newspaper that his mother really enjoyed. The ad was asking for people to sell the paper, so Joel signed it and sent it in. The company started mailing him bundles of papers that arrived on Thursdays to be sold on Saturday. Early each Saturday morning Joel headed for West Monroe with his bicycle basket filled with newspapers. There he sold *The Grit* on the street for a dime. He also found a nice residential area and sold the papers, house-to-house, and developed a few regular customers. He got to keep a nickle out of every dime he collected, and sent the other nickle to the company. Joel took his job seriously. He felt responsible for those who were depending on him, and he delivered their newspaper come rain or shine.

One Saturday he was too sick with the flu to make his rounds. His dad knew how important this job was to Joel. He had customers counting on him, and he didn't want to let them down. So Dad took Raymond in the car, and they delivered the paper to Joel's regular customers to help him fulfill his obligation.

Joel gave up selling *The Grit* after a few weeks because he encountered a lot of indifference that took the heart out of him. He found wealthy people to whom a dime would have meant nothing, who had no problem saying "no" to a kid on a bicycle who was working hard, trying to make a little spending money. The indifference that he experienced made a lasting impression on him. To this day, he can't pass up a child who has something to sell, even if he has no use for it. The struggles, hopes and dreams of children touch Joel's heart and stir his compassion. He understands their feelings because he's been there.

The Taxidermist
Joel was always ready to expand his horizons and was interested in developing new skills. At one point he decided to become a taxidermist. He found an ad in the paper where he could order a ten-week course to learn the art for a dollar a week, so he ordered the course. The first lesson came, and he was supposed to kill a bird or small animal. They showed with diagrams how to skin the creature, then use alum and salt to preserve the skin, and then he was to keep it until lesson number two came.

Birds were plentiful, and at certain times of the year during migration, they blackened the sky and filled the pastures. Joel and Dan shot birds whenever they wanted to. But the hunter's rule was that you had to eat whatever you killed; it couldn't be wasted. They killed black birds, robins, and crows and dressed them out, and Mom Hemphill would fry them. The boys were proud of their hunting skills and found the birds to be good eating.

So when taxidermy lesson number one came, Joel got his gun and started looking for a bird. Sure enough one lit on the electric wire in front of the house, and he shot it. He didn't know that his dad was watching from a distance. When he picked up the bird and started toward the house, Dad stopped him and said, "Son what are you going to do with that bird?" Joel answered, "I'm learning how to be a taxidermist and I'm going to mount it."

Dad, who was a very compassionate man and himself quite a hunter, said with a sad look on his face and a tear in his voice, "Son, are you telling me that you killed that little bird just for his hide?" "Yes sir," Joel replied weakly. Dad turned and walked away without further comment, but he had said enough to take all the shine off of Joel's career as a taxidermist. It didn't take him long to write the company a note telling them that he did not wish to continue the course and requesting them not to send the next lesson. The company ignored Joel's letter, and the packets kept coming, along with threatening letters stating that if he didn't catch up on his payments, he was going to be sued.

This ongoing correspondence with the taxidermy company became Joel's troublesome secret. It was a nightmare that caused him to lie awake in dread and fear. Finally he went to his mother for help. Mama was very understanding and said, "Son, don't worry about it anymore. I'll take care of it." She wrote the company a letter and explained that Joel was just a ten-year-old boy, and they wouldn't have any success with a lawsuit. She also said that she would pay them what he rightfully owed, and that put a stop to the harassing letters. As far as Joel knows, they never heard from the company again.

Politics

In 1950 when he was eleven, Joel finally landed a job. It came about when their congressman, Otto Passman, was running for re-election and was scheduled to speak in Bawcomville at Lenwil School. Mr. Passman was a well-liked businessman who owned a furniture store in downtown Monroe. *Passman's Supply* was a large thriving business that sold office furniture as well as furnishings for the household. Joel's mother and dad liked Mr. Passman and wanted him to remain in office. He was a conservative, as were most of the people of their area of northeast Louisiana, and ever since he had helped Bawcomville obtain the ring levee, he was more than a politician to the Hemphills, he was a friend.

Shady Wall, a young debonair businessman and upcoming politician was their state representative in Baton Rouge. Shady, who was known as a ladies' man, was also a flaming liberal and surrounded himself with other like-minded young men. Even though it was illegal, he had been caught at a motel gambling and was charged. Of course all of this was well known and was covered extensively by the media. It was the news of the day.

Joel's Dad certainly didn't feel like this young liberal was anyone whom they needed representing their district in Washington. So when Shady challenged Mr. Passman for the Congressional office, Dad supported Passman. The Hemphill children were well versed on the two candidates, as the subject was a favorite around the dinner table. And Mom had her opinion about politicians because she kept up with them through the newspaper.

Both candidates held political rallies and speaking engagements before groups in different communities. They did all kinds of things to draw crowds, featuring country music being the most effective. It was a common thing in Louisiana for politicians to hire live bands for entertainment to help gather the people. In fact, Louisiana had even elected a well known country singer by the name of Jimmy Davis as Governor. He was well respected and stayed in office for two terms.

Joel and Anna Gayle were walking to Lenwil School to Mr. Passman's rally one evening and were all excited. There was to be a musical band and free ice cream in abundance. But on the way, one of Shady Wall's men drove by them in a white panel truck with the candidate's picture on the sides. The truck was ominous looking with big loud speaker horns mounted on top.

When they saw him nailing Shady Wall posters to the electric poles they were aggravated and followed along behind him taking them down. Being just children, they didn't understand that he was within his rights to nail them up. To them, he was on their territory and shouldn't be doing this in the area and on the day of Mr. Passman's rally. Their family was not for Mr. Wall for good reasons, and they certainly didn't want him canvassing Bawcomville for votes. So Joel and Gayle took action the only way they knew how.

When the man in the panel truck came back around and caught them taking his posters down, he stopped, and in a nice way, asked them why they were doing that. Joel spoke up and said, "Because we are against Shady Wall." When asked why, Joel answered, "He is too young and inexperienced to be a Congressman. The newspaper said that he even stood up in

Baton Rouge and said 'I'm Shady Wall and I'm the next Huey Long'." Joel said he thought those words were ridiculous and had finished him off for Louisiana and the Hemphills! Shady Wall had shown what a novice he was to compare himself to the famous Kingfish, and Joel was quick to point that out. Huey P. Long, even though he was controversial, had brought Louisiana out of the backwoods with new highways and bridges, and a better educational system. He was their hero. Many politicians reached for Huey Long's status and would like to have filled that position, but the Hemphills believed that Shady Wall was not going to be that man!

Joel and Anna Gayle nicely gave the man in the white panel truck an earful, and after they said their piece, he had no more questions and quietly drove off. The two of them went on to the school house and enjoyed the music, the speech, and of course, ice cream. After it was over, Joel was surprised when his dad came up to him and said, "Mr. Passman wants to see you." When Joel stood before Otto Passman, he was impressed by the tall distinguished looking congressman.

Mr. Passman was friendly and greeted Joel warmly, and then told him that he had heard about his encounter with Mr. Wall's worker in the white panel truck. He assured Joel that he sincerely appreciated his speaking up for him and his enthusiastic support, but tearing down another candidate's posters wasn't the proper way to do it. He went on to say, "If you would like to help me, come by my office the first of the week and we'll get started." That's when Joel landed his first job. He immediately went to work for Mr. Passman, walking around town distributing handbills to shoppers and putting them in car windows or under wiper blades. When it came time to vote, Joel also stood at the polls, handing out literature and at other times, walked down the streets wearing Passman posters. As far as Joel was concerned, this was the most rewarding job that he could have, and the pay was great. One day he made eleven dollars which was unheard of for a boy his age. And the job continued off and on for several years.

In 1952 when Ike Eisenhower, who was a Republican, ran against Adlai Stevenson, a Democrat, for president, Mr. Passman hired Joel and his buddies to canvass downtown Monroe for the Democratic nominee. Joel's dad and family, along with most of northeast Louisiana, was for Eisenhower, but out of loyalty to Mr. Passman, Joel and his buddies covered Monroe with Stevenson literature. That was his first bitter taste of being unpopular. In some people's minds he was working for the wrong side, and they didn't fail to let him know it.

Through the years Dad and Otto Passman remained dear friends and kept up correspondence, either by phone or mail. When Brother Hemphill would hear from Passman, he would always ask about Joel and comment on what a fine young man he was.

When Joel graduated from high school, Mr. Passman wrote him a nice letter of commendation. Then he called Dad and offered Joel an appointment to West Point. At that time, Passman was likely the most powerful man in Congress. Committee chairmanships are based on seniority, and he had been re-elected again and again, and thus became chairman of the *House Appropriations Subcommittee* on foreign aid. With his powerful position he could have easily arranged the appointment if Joel had been inclined to have a career in the military. Joel's older brother Dubb had chosen that path and was very successful as an officer in the Air Force. Mr. Passman's offer was not taken lightly by Joel. He felt honored by it, but in his heart he knew that was not where he was headed. Even though he didn't know where he was going, he knew that it wasn't the military, and he has never been sorry for his decision.

Chapter Six

Pastor W.T. Hemphill

Pastor W. T. Hemphill

W.T. Hemphill was a true man of God and the founding pastor of the *Jesus Only Apostolic Church* in 1944. He was a stocky built man of Scots-Irish and German descent, and stood about 5 feet 10 inches tall. He had an abundance of black hair and his dark brown eyes spoke with a twinkle.

Dad Hemphill, born December 10, 1892, was up in years when Joel and his younger siblings came along, but was a physically strong man in spite of his age. Even though he was a man of the cloth, a teacher of the Word with a thriving church, he never stopped working with his hands as long as his health allowed. He was a carpenter by trade and carried a union card until his demise at the age of 88. He loved to build. He seemed to always be building something, and to Mom's dismay had storage sheds behind and to the side of the house. She wasn't as proud of "those old sheds" as he was and thought they cluttered up the place.

In Joel's earlier years, Dad not only was a carpenter, a painter and paper hanger, but also a well digger. He dug wells by hand, and Joel's older brothers, W.T. Junior, better known as "Dubb," and Daniel, helped him. They would roll a big concrete culvert section and set it where they were going to dig, and as the hole grew big enough that section would slide down into it. The older brothers kept the hole free of loose dirt by drawing it out in a bucket tied with a rope, much like you'd draw water. When each section would slide down into the ground, even with the surface, another one was rolled into place on top of it. It was backbreaking work, and they continued digging until the well was about forty feet deep. They would usually hit seep water at about twenty feet and that's when the work got messy and tricky. A few times they hit the main stream before they expected to, and it was all they could do to get out before the well filled up with water.

Man Of Prayer
Dad Hemphill was a praying man who walked in covenant relationship with the Lord and had many miracles during his ministry. His usual daily routine included early morning prayer, beginning before daylight, with trips to the barn for prayer two or more times during the day. Joel remembers seeing the calluses on his dad's knees from spending so much time in prayer. The neighbors who lived close by, including those who weren't church-going Christians, could hear him pray, and at times, commented on how it comforted them, especially during tornado season.

Joel's dad was easily recognized on his daily rounds to the hospitals, the post office, and the places of business that he frequented. He wore a hat and never went to town without it. It mattered not about the weather, how hot and humid it was, Dad would be fully dressed in a two piece suit, white shirt and tie, with his *Jesus Only* pin attached near the top. He carried himself with an air of dignity at a brisk pace. Brother W.T. Hemphill was a compassionate man with a good sense of humor and was loved and respected, not only by his family and the members of his church, but by people throughout the twin cities. He was known for being a man of his word and prompt in paying his bills. Another thing that he was known and loved for was his

Pastor W.T. Hemphill

success in rescuing young men from the Louisiana Training Institute (L.T.I.), and even prison. Many of these boys who were in trouble with the law had no one who cared. Brother Hemphill cared, and because he did, there were some who received a better chance in life through his efforts.

Kenny Chilton was one of those young men and wrote his testimony in a letter to Joel several years ago. In his own words he tells how he was blessed through Dad's ministry and the Bawcomville church, after he gave his heart to the Lord in a church in Winnsboro. Kenny says:

> *"I started attending Jesus Only Apostolic Church shortly thereafter. I had been going to your Dad's church about a month when I got a letter in the mail from the Louisiana Department of Motor Vehicles, stating that I was being sued for $1,000.00.*
>
> *The reason was, I had a wreck in New Orleans before I got in church, and if I didn't pay the $1,000.00 they were going to take my driver's license. I had just gone to work at Monroe Bearing, driving a delivery truck at $1.60 per hour. Needless to say $1,000.00 was like $1,000,000.00 to me. As you know, I had just gotten out of the Louisiana State Penitentiary at Angola after being locked up for five years. I was locked up in Louisiana, New Mexico, Arizona, California, Washington, Oregon, and Canada. The states of Louisiana and Oregon had declared me criminally insane with a criminal profile,*

and that I would probably be imprisoned most of my life. When I got the letter from the state, I was living with my mother and it seemed like all hell was turned loose on me. I felt totally defeated and that it would only be a matter of time before I was back on the street. Then I got a phone call that was so astounding, I'll never forget it as long as I live.

Brother Hemphill called me and told me that the Lord Jesus had showed him that one of his sheep was in trouble, and would I mind meeting him over at his house. At this time I didn't personally know your Dad because I had only been attending church about a month, and Brother Hemphill didn't know me either, although he knew I had been in prison for five years and that I had recently started attending the church he pastored. The only people that knew of the lawsuit were my Mother and I, and she didn't go to church at all. It still astounds me when I think of it. I went over to Brother Hemphill's house and we sat in the swing at the end of the carport. He reached in his pocket and pulled out a cashier's check made out to Kenny Chilton, for $1,000.00. He then told me that if I could pay the money back, it would be good, but he said if for any reason I couldn't pay it back, that would be good too. There is no way I can explain how that affected me. Your Dad *still is the greatest person I have ever known. I thank God that I was able to sit under his ministry for his last years. It took me awhile, but I finally paid it all back. After I had been paying him awhile, he called me aside at church one night and said, 'Brother Kenny, I haven't been keeping record, but it seems like you shouldn't owe me but about $100.00 more.' I told him that I was keeping a record and that I still owed him $600.00.*

Sister Hemphill started encouraging me to go back to school and finish high school. I went to night school and after a few months, I received my GED. After this your Mother told me that I needed to check into getting a full pardon from the state of Louisiana, and having my criminal record cleared. She said I needed to look ahead to a job, marriage and family, and that she and Brother Hemphill would help in any way they could. I didn't have any money, so I went to the Department of Corrections Office of Probation and Parole. I filled out a standard application, which if you didn't have any money, usually got lost in the shuffle. Brother Hemphill went and talked to some attorneys, and each lawyer told him the same thing. I had a bad record, I had not been out of prison very long and it took a lot of money, of which I had none.

> *This was in the early part of the year (1974). Over in the summer of the same year Brother Hemphill called me aside at church one night and told me that he had written a letter to Governor Edwin Edwards, petitioning him for a full pardon for me. He also told me that he told Governor Edwards that he had personally tried me and that I had passed the test with flying colors. The test he was referring to was when he was going to let me out of the debt for $100.00, when I really owed him $600.00 on the $1,000.00 he gave me with no strings attached. In September of 1974 Brother Hemphill again called me aside and told me that the Lord showed him I would have the pardon before Christmas of the same year (1974). At this time I was living in a garage apartment on Austin Avenue in West Monroe. Christmas came and went with no pardon. January 1975 came and went with no pardon, then February 1975 and no pardon."*

Kenny says that at this point he was tempted to doubt the prophecy, or that Brother Hemphill had heard from God. However, he says:

> *"Then I came home from work one day in March and there was a large manilla envelope in my mailbox. I saw it was from the office of the governor. Sure enough, it was my full pardon with restoration of citizenship and the right to own and posses a*

firearm. A convicted felon loses his citizenship, can't vote or own a gun, and cannot hold a public trust job. All of that had been wiped clean. Sister Hemphill said that God had forgiven me, then He got man to forgive me. The most powerful thing of all was when I looked at the bottom of the pardon. It had the Governor's gold seal and it said, 'Signed and on record this day by the honorable Governor Edwin Edwards, December 19, 1974!' So I had the pardon on December 19, 1974, six days before Christmas!

Not a day goes by that I don't call the Hemphill's names in prayer. I'm not called to preach, teach, or any of the five-fold ministry, etc., but Jesus chose one of the biggest abject failures that ever was and called him to be a Christian and for this I'm eternally grateful. For twenty-nine years when the battle gets to be too much, I go to Isaiah 28:11-12; "For with stammering lips and another tongue will he speak to this people. To whom he said, "This is the rest wherewith ye may cause the weary to rest; and this is the refreshing." Your Mom and Dad, along with all the saints of Jesus Only Apostolic Church, took me under their wing and showed me by example that I, a total failure, could make it all the way. I hope this

> *means as much to you as the experience of it means to me. I believe it will."*
> *In Jesus Name,*
> *Brother Kenny Chilton*

That letter says it all. Kenny did go on with his life. He married a lovely Christian girl, and he and Janice are faithful members of the Bawcomville church today. He became a valued employee of the General Motors Guide Plant, a loving husband and father, and a credit to society. All Kenny needed was a chance, and God gave him that chance through a devoted pastor and a loving and caring church.

There are many wonderful testimonies from the days of Dad's ministry. Another one concerns a young man named Aaron Bouwel who was in need of a job. The church had been praying that he would find work, and what seemed like an answer to prayer soon came along. Aaron's older brother was working in south Louisiana for an offshore drilling company. He had spoken to his boss about Aaron and landed him a job. Aaron knew that the work in Louisiana's *Outer Continental Shelf (OCS)* territory in the Gulf of Mexico was dangerous, but the money was good.

Millions of acres of OFC land off Louisiana's coast were set aside for oil speculation back in 1950, and large companies were taking advantage of their right to drill. But they needed men who were willing to take the risk of explosions, rough waters, and hurricanes, and they were paying large salaries to recruit them. Hurricanes posed the greatest threat and the oil companies were constantly trying to design a safety device for their crew members. That's how the "survival capsule" came into being.

Someone described it as resembling a flying saucer with portholes. The capsule was equipped with a diesel engine and a five-day supply of marine rations. It also had hand-held distress flares, signal pistols, and compressed air for the crew to breath, if needed, while sailing through flames from a burning rig.

Aware of the danger involved, Aaron came to his pastor on Sunday afternoon around one o'clock for advice. When he asked Brother Hemphill what he thought about him taking the job, he said "Brother Aaron, give me a couple of days to pray about it." But Aaron said "Brother Hemphill, I don't have that much time, they're leaving today at three o'clock this afternoon." Dad studied for a few minutes then said, "Here is how I feel in my spirit. Don't go this time. Wait and go next time." Aaron took his pastor's advice and stayed behind that afternoon when his brother left for the coast. A few days later the Bawcomville church was stunned at the grim headlines that read, ***"13 Die As Oil-Rig Rescue Fails In Gulf."*** The first paragraph of the article said, *"A survival capsule from a sinking oil-drilling rig flipped over early today during a storm in the Gulf of Mexico and thirteen men trapped inside died."* One of those men was Aaron Bouwel's brother, and this is the rig that he would have been on!

Another great testimony came about when Howard and Vestal Goodman were staying with the Hemphills while preaching a revival for them. Their children were very young at that time and five-year-old Vickie had suffered severely with asthma for all of her life. She and Joel's little sister Brenda were out in the yard one day, playing in the sandbox, and Vickie was struggling so hard to breath that her head was wet with perspiration. Brother Hemphill, who was outside also, came by and noticed her labored breathing. Vestal happened to be watching from the house and saw Dad take off his hat, look toward heaven and start praying. Then he had both children raise their hands in the air, and he placed his hands on Vickie's head and prayed. Everyone was amazed when they realized that Vickie was completely healed, and from that day on she never had another asthma attack! Howard and Vestal talked about that miracle through the years.

Patsy Guess was another little girl from the Bawcomville assembly who had a great miracle. She became the victim of a horrible accident as she was about to cross the Jonesboro road while going to Jackson's store one evening, before church, and was hit by a big truck traveling at a fast rate of speed. Seven-year-old Patsy was struck with such force that it knocked her out of her shoes and she was thrown about sixty feet and landed in a road ditch that was partially filled with water. The violent impact caused the truck driver to slam on his breaks with horrific sounds of screeching tires and the smell of burning rubber as the truck finally came to a stop. Those that witnessed the accident started running and screaming, some toward Patsy and others toward the church to inform her family and Brother Hemphill. It was utter chaos. The on-lookers believed that Patsy must be dead. No one could survive that kind of brutal force.

When the news reached Dad, he along with her family rushed to the scene. Dad, in his new white suit that Mom had bought him for Easter, waded off into the water where Patsy was lying. It seemed hopeless! She was ashen and lifeless, but Dad fell on his knees there in the mud and started calling on the name of Jesus. A nurse soon arrived and pronounced the child "dead" and someone covered her up. It was easy to see that her little body was broken beyond repair and lifeless, but Dad kept on praying and crying out to the Lord. He just wouldn't give up. One elder of the church who was a witness says, "I watched Brother Hemphill with a Niagra of tears streaming down his face, call Patsy's life back into her body." This witness says that Patsy showed no signs of life until Dad, continuing to pray, began speaking in tongues. "She coughed and then was noticeably alive." By the time the ambulance got her to the emergency room she was breathing but far from out of danger. Days went by and the physicians still refused to set her bones, concerned that she wouldn't survive the shock. Some said that even if Patsy lived she would be a cripple for the rest of her life. But Dad and the church kept praying for her. He said the Lord had assured him that she would pull through, and he kept encouraging the family that she would live and be whole again. And that is exactly what happened! Patsy is alive today, normal and healthy! She and her husband recently went on a cruise to Hawaii to celebrate 38 years of marriage.

Dad Loved To Sing
Brother Hemphill loved to sing. He sang when he was happy and he sang when he was sad. He could sing every verse and line of some of the saddest songs ever written: "tear-jerkers" like *"Baggage Coach Ahead," "Little Girl In The Snow,"* and *"My Angel Mother's Grave."* He owned one of the finest *Martin D28* guitars, and though he couldn't play it, he had several children who could. He usually had a guitar pick in his pocket because when he got ready to sing he wanted someone to strum rhythm for him. After Juanita left home, Joel was usually that someone. Later in life, it wasn't unusual to see him in the back yard swing under the shade trees, and to hear him singing one of those sad songs, his hat in his hand and tears in his eyes.

When his granddaughter, Candy, was approaching her teens, she and her little cousin, Rachel, came upon Dad in the swing with moist eyes singing *My Angel Mother's Grave*. Six-year-old Rachael looked up at Candy with tears in her eyes and blurted out, "He's missing his mother!" There was no way of knowing what was going on in his heart and mind when he sang those old songs. Dad had already lived a full and eventful life before he married Joel's mother, and the family had heard him tell of his many experiences while pioneering the Pentecostal message.

The Early Ministry of Brother Hemphill
Brother Hemphill began his ministry as a Holiness Methodist, and at the same time was a minister of the *Salvation Army*. This international organization was founded in England by William Booth in 1865 as a religious and philanthropic movement for the very poor and was already doing a great work in the United States in the early 1900's.

In 1912, at the age of 20, Brother Hemphill was in Fort Worth, Texas for a *Salvation Army* meeting. While he was there, he came upon a big tent where someone was having a revival, so he attended. He listened intently as they preached with enthusiasm about the baptism with the Holy Spirit. This was new to him, and after he returned to his room, he began to search the Scriptures. As he did, he became convinced that what they were preaching was true and it was an experience for Christians today. The next time he attended the tent meeting, it was with a great hunger for that experience. His plan was to go to the altar that night and ask God for the in-filling, but the service lasted long. He couldn't wait any longer for them to give the invitation so he went back to his hotel room and knelt by his bed and began to pray and ask the Lord to fill him with the Holy Ghost. In a few minutes, still dressed in his Salvation Army uniform, he found himself gloriously baptized with joy and speaking in tongues!

Dad was never the same after that. He had found the *"exceeding great joy"* that the Apostles refer to over and over in the Scriptures. It was like *"fire shut up in his bones" (Jer. 20:9)*.

> *"I indeed baptize you with water unto repentance: but he who cometh after me is mightier than I, whose shoes I am not worthy to bear: he shall **baptize you with the Holy Ghost and with fire**"* [John the Baptist speaking] *(Matt. 3:11)*.
>
> *"...how much more shall your heavenly Father give the Holy Spirit to them that **ask him**?" (Luke 11:13)*.

When Dad Hemphill was baptized with the Holy Ghost, he received what old-timers referred to as the "go-tell-it." He, along with his wife Etta, soon gathered up a band of believers with the same experience and zeal and started going from town to town, preaching wherever he could. Sometimes it was in a country schoolhouse or on someone's front porch. The people would gather, drawn by the dynamic preaching and singing.

Brush Arbors
In some places they set up "brush arbors" to have service. This was done by setting poles in the ground, placing poles across the top, and then adding brush. The brush was for shade from the sun in the day and to help keep the dew out at night. The men would then go to the sawmill and haul wagon loads of slabs and blocks to make benches. Slabs were long strips of logs with the bark still on one side. On the other side the slab was smooth

because that's where the mill started cutting boards. The blocks were short ends of logs that were also rejects. From these materials they fashioned rough, backless benches. Then they gathered wagon loads of sawdust and scattered it on the ground for the floor. It was a resourceful way of having a quick, makeshift church without much cost; therefore it wasn't hard to leave behind when the *Hemphill Band* decided it was time to move on. Later on, tents were used with similar furnishings.

There is much to be said about the early days of the Holiness movement. Those old brush arbor and tent revivals had a compelling atmosphere. Kerosene lanterns were hung on nails driven into the poles, and the sweet smell of fresh-cut lumber and sawdust chips permeated the air, all of which added to the excitement. It seemed like more evidence that something fresh and new had arrived, and no one wanted to miss it, so people gathered in great numbers.

Joel's dad became a trailblazer, and it wasn't easy. He really wasn't preaching anything new; it was just new to those to whom he was sent. It was the same as in the Bible days when Aquila and Priscilla went to hear Apollos preach, as recorded in the book of Acts.

> *"This man was instructed in the way of the Lord; and, being fervent in the spirit, he spoke and taught diligently the things of the Lord, **knowing only the baptism of John**...whom when Aquila and Priscilla had heard, they took unto them and expounded unto him **the way of God more perfectly**" (Acts 18:25-26).*

The apostle Paul found more of John's converts in Ephesus and asked them an interesting question:

> *"He said unto them,* ***Have ye received the Holy Ghost since ye believed****? And they said unto him, We have not so much as heard whether there is any Holy Ghost. And he said unto them, What, then, were ye baptized? And they said, Unto John's baptism" (Acts 19:2-3).*

When they heard Paul's message about the baptism of the Holy Spirit, they desired that he baptize them in water again:

> *"When they heard this, they were baptized in the name of the Lord Jesus" (v. 5).*

> *"And when Paul had laid his hands upon them,* ***the Holy Ghost came on them, and they spoke with tongues, and prophesied****" (v. 6).*

By these Scriptures it's easy to see that the message of "Jesus name baptism," and receiving an in-filling of the Holy Spirit has been around since the second chapter of Acts. But like Paul and the rest of the Apostles, anyone who **introduces** unfamiliar truths has to pay the price.

Dad Hemphill wasn't just called to preach; he was called to suffer. He was one of the early pioneers of a new spiritual awakening. Not everyone received it gladly, and he found himself much like Paul:

> *"...for he is a chosen vessel unto me, to bear my name before the Gentiles...I will show*

> him how great things he must **suffer** for my name's sake" (Acts 9:15-16).

And suffer he did. But great things are birthed through suffering. Our founding fathers who heard the call to establish a new country with freedom of worship and a better way of life, also heard the call to suffer. John Adams shows his pain in a letter to his beloved wife Abigail, dated April 26, 1777. He was homesick and weary with trying to help craft a government *"for the people."* He had fought loneliness for years to the point of despair while facing the uncertainties of the Revolutionary War. He cried out in distress in his letter to her:

> *"Posterity! You will never know how much it cost the present generation to preserve your freedom! I hope you will make a good use of it. If you do not, I shall repent in heaven that I ever took half the pains to preserve it." (John Adams; "My Dearest Friend." p. 171).*

Traveling By Wagon

In 1915 Brother Hemphill pulled into a Louisiana campground in a mule drawn wagon in search of someone to return with him to a nearby town and assist in a revival. When Dad arrived, the campground was vacant, the meeting had closed, and everyone had gone except several young men. Brother Oliver Fauss was just starting as a young minister at the time and wrote a book about his experiences. In his book he describes what happened when Dad showed up that day.

> *"Everyone had returned to his home. Everyone that is, except a few of us young men who for some unknown reason felt led to*

stay behind. For the next three days we made it a daily practice to retreat to the woods for lengthy prayer meetings, in which we would plead with the Lord to show us His will in our lives. The fourth day a man drove into the campground from a sawmill camp about twenty miles away. He said he was looking for Gospel workers to accompany him back to the camp for a tent meeting he was planning. We felt that this was the answer to prayers, so the next morning, the six of us accompanied him in his rough-riding wagon. Our combined finances consisted of forty-five cents and a few postage stamps. After a few hours of bumpy riding along the dusty Louisiana roads, we stopped for lunch and spent our forty-five cents. Imagine feeding seven grown men for forty-five cents. But, you could buy a lot of crackers for forty-five cents at a country store in 1915."

Brother Fauss continues:

"After several hours of bumpy riding, and eating dust we arrived in one of the most out-of-the-way places I have ever visited. I was sure that we were in the middle of the jungle...It took us four days to erect the tent and make preparations for the revival. While we worked, we prayed and sang. Just the thought that God had sent us here to do a work for Him was enough to keep us happy.

> *....I'll not say much about our meals those first few days, as there's not much to discuss. One evening (we all) shared a can of peaches and two boxes of crackers. Mother was not there with hot biscuits, so I had to learn to enjoy cornbread and syrup."*

Brother Fauss tells of the success of that revival and of preaching his very first sermon. It was on a Monday afternoon while in prayer and Bible study when he felt that the Lord had given him a message for that evening's service. He writes:

> *"The workers would spend hours each day out in the woods seeking the will of the Lord, and praying that souls would be saved in our services."* He continues. *"...the Lord revealed to me that He wanted me to preach my message in service that night. I said, 'I will Lord, but You'll have to instruct Brother Hemphill to ask me, as he is our leader.' Sure enough, that night at service time, Brother Hemphill came up to me and said, 'Brother Oliver, I feel that the Lord would have you preach for us tonight. When it came time to preach, I took a deep breath and nervously stepped out in front of what appeared to me as the biggest crowd of people I had ever seen."*

Obviously this beginning of Brother Fauss' preaching ministry was ordained of God, as he says, *"the altar was filled with hungry seekers almost as soon as the invitation was given."*

Brother Fauss went on in evangelistic and pastoral ministry for over sixty years and had phenomenal success.

His account of those early years didn't vary from Dad's. The revival fires blazed through the south and were fueled by prayer, dedication, and a desire to see people saved, no matter what the cost!

The 1915 Revival in Pollock
In that same year, Brother Hemphill went to Pollock, Louisiana, where he had grown up, and where his dad and mother still lived, for another Gospel meeting. The results were more than he could have hoped for. In six weeks of services, scores repented of their sins and were baptized, and ninety received an in-filling of the Holy Ghost. People were miraculously saved, healed, and set free. But when you have a great move of God, you always have some who are not happy about it. The *evil one* stirred up otherwise good men to do wicked things in that town to crush people's spirits and quell the revival fires that burned in their midst. They used harsh methods of force and cruelty. Some of them roughly ordered Dad to leave the area, but his reply was "I'll leave when my Father tells me to." Those angry men went away shaking their heads saying, "That preacher sure honors his dad." But Dad was referring to his Heavenly Father, not Tilman Beauregard, his earthly father. The next thing those men did was show up in one of the services.

The night they came, the meeting was packed as usual. When the altar call was given, a couple of the trouble-makers had devised a scheme. They would go and kneel at the altar, pretending to pray. One of them had "brass knucks" on his hand, just waiting for Dad to come pray with him. When Dad knelt down beside him, the man came up with his fist and the "brass knucks" and hit Dad in the face. The blow almost knocked him out and did break his nose and loosen his front teeth. When one of the church brethren saw Dad with blood streaming down his face and dripping onto his white shirt, he stepped up, took Dad by the arm, and led him through the crowd. Dad said that several men were there to back up the man who assaulted him, but when the Christian brother came and took Dad by the arm, the crowd parted and let them through. Dad believed that the Lord blinded their eyes, because they were there to really work him over. He was sure they would never have let him go otherwise.

Knowing about the trouble, but not seeing his son leave, grandfather T.B. went searching for him. When he went home and found that he wasn't there, he started back across town to the meeting place. By then the group of men had become an angry mob. When they spotted T.B., they beat him mercilessly, broke several of his ribs, and threw him into a pile of brush. They were still under the impression that this was the *father* that wouldn't let Dad leave town.

Through the years when Dad Hemphill recalled those days, it always brought tears to his eyes and pain in his heart. He would say, "That was the greatest trial of my life. I was tempted to get a shotgun, find those men, and handle their actions in a fleshly manner. I wanted to give them a dose of their own medicine." By the grace of God, Dad soon overcame those feelings, and rose above their demeaning tactics. As a result, there is a thriving Full Gospel church today on the very spot where that dynamic revival took place so many years ago.

Pastor W.T. Hemphill

No Automobiles
Brother W.T. Hemphill's ministry began before the days of automobiles. There was little entertainment at home, so everyone went to the *Holy Roller* meetings to hear the music, the singing and preaching, and see who they could see. There were drums, tambourines, accordions, guitars and heartfelt singing in abundance. The preachers preached a mainline Christian message which was salvation *only* through the blood of Jesus. They preached hell hot, heaven real and eternity long, and baptized their converts in water in Jesus name. They laid hands on the sick and multitudes were saved, healed, and baptized with the Holy Ghost. When Dad and his band went to a town, it wasn't unusual for their meetings to shut down the bars and cinemas. Those tent revivals and brush arbor meetings were where the excitement was, and tremendous crowds came. Dad remembers the attendance being so large in one small town that when he gave the altar call, people came down in such numbers that he could not move from where he was standing, so he had to kneel right were he had preached.

The Newspaper Article
Those brush arbor and tent revival meetings caused such a stir in the south that the *Times Picayune* of New Orleans sent a reporter out to some of the services to get a story, without Dad's knowledge. By then T.B. had passed away and Brother Hemphill's mother, Willie Anna was living in Shreveport with her youngest son, Cornelius, and his family. They were surprised to find a syndicated article describing Dad's meetings in their Shreveport paper. They sent the newspaper clipping to Dad and it read something like this: "Each night throngs of people come out to the meetings in wagons, on bicycles, horseback, and on foot." The reporter went on to tell about the

powerful preaching and singing and called Dad *"the Apostle and High Priest of the Holy Rollers."* Dad found this amusing and always chuckled when he reminisced about that newspaper article, as that was nothing he would have thought of claiming for himself.

More Threats and Hardtimes
In those early days, there were times when Dad was shot at and rotten egged as he preached behind the pulpit. He said that when the hecklers ran out of rotten eggs, they threw fresh ones, and some would land unbroken in the wood shavings. After the service, Etta and the other women would gather the eggs that didn't break and cook them for super. Being bombarded with rotten eggs and tomatoes was small compared to the many times his life was threatened. He remembered an occasion when, as he walked down the street of one town where he was preaching, a man of large stature, who owned a hardware store, came up beside him. He continued to walk along with Dad with his fist doubled up cursing and threatening him. He said "There is a group of us men who are not going to allow you to continue preaching the Holy Roller message in this town." When Dad started to say something the man stopped him and warned, "Don't open your mouth or I will stomp you into this sidewalk. If you are not out of town by Friday, we are going to string you up to one of these power poles."

Dad didn't leave town, and of course the lynching didn't take place, but the threat caused him and his co-workers to pray more fervently. Dad loved the south but knew that era was notorious for hangings. In a period of several years, there were some 3000 lynchings of both blacks and whites. People were hanged who were guilty of a crime, or just breaking some social code, such as

Pastor W.T. Hemphill

preaching the gospel. If God hadn't protected Dad in those days, he could easily have been among that number.

In recalling the events of his early ministry, Dad often told about the incident of the kerosene lantern that hung on a pole near the Bible stand. It was always necessary to have one there for the reading of the Word. One night when the service was called to order, all of the believers came forward to kneel and pray. While kneeling at the Bible stand, he had a vision of the lantern falling and hitting him on the head. When he got up from prayer, he summoned a couple of the elders, told them his vision and asked them to please make sure the lantern was securely fastened so it wouldn't fall. This they did. Later on in the service, the vision was forgotten, but while Dad was preaching, the lantern fell striking him on the head. It caused a cut and bleeding and produced a scar that he wore for the rest of his life. The only explanation for the vision in Dad's mind was that it was given to strengthen their faith. He felt that God was letting them know that He could reveal the future whenever He wanted to.

There were usually eight to ten members in Dad's gospel band when they went into a town for revival: perhaps another couple with small children, along with one or two single young men, then Dad, his wife Etta, and two or three of their children. Their routine when not holding street meetings during the day was to pass the time with one hour in prayer, one hour of Bible study, and one hour of recreation. The latter was spent by taking a walk or talking and visiting.

Money was scarce, so no one had much, especially to give in the offerings; mostly it was just a few pennies. But a local baker who was friendly to their message donated all the bread they wanted, and a man from the flour mill donated flour. So they had light bread and flour gravy for breakfast and flour gravy and light bread for supper. Though Dad appreciated something to eat, he got so burned out on light bread that he would hardly eat it in his later years, preferring biscuits or cornbread. He referred to light bread as "punk."

Fed By A German Shepherd
One morning after Bible study and prayer, Dad and several of the brethren were standing outside the dwelling tents where there was a railroad track and a dirt road which was little more than a path. As they were talking, their attention was drawn to a large dog with a package in his mouth coming toward them. One of the men said, "What is that dog carrying?" When the dog got even with them, he dropped the package and never stopped. He just kept trotting on. They went over and picked it up and found it to be two nice round steaks, wrapped in butcher paper and perfectly covered. They could hardly believe their eyes, but their next meal was *steak*, gravy and light bread! There was much rejoicing around the table that day. They enjoyed their delicious meal and ate it gladly, giving thanks to the Lord. They were convinced that the God of heaven had sent meat to them by a German Shepherd dog, just as He sent *"bread and meat"* by the ravens to feed Elijah by the brook Cherith *(I Kings 17:3-6)*.

Much more could be written on Brother W.T. Hemphill's experiences in those early years, including how he was a member of some ten so called "Oneness" organizations, several of which he helped to found. *"Oneness"* is the belief that Jesus Christ is the human incarnation of God the Father. Shortly after being baptized with the Holy Spirit and being associated with

Pastor W.T. Hemphill

Pentecostal brethren at camp-meetings, he began to question why they weren't baptizing their converts in *Jesus' name* as the apostles did. *(Acts 2:38; 8:16; 10:48; 19:5)*. The doctrine of the *trinity* was another troubling idea that he couldn't find Scripture to back up. He was an avid Bible reader and spent hours in Bible study and prayer, and these issues became paramount to him and a few of his associates.

The Division
Dad was at the camp meeting in Hot Springs, Arkansas in 1914 when the division came. Those who held to the doctrine of three-in-one in their interpretation of *Matthew 28:19*, started the *Assemblies of God* denomination. Dad and several other brethren pulled away and after months of Bible study and discussion, started what is known as the *Jesus Only* movement. As unfortunate as this division might have been for the Pentecostal cause, it remains one of the realities of our time.

The Oneness movement of today can be traced to that time period. Dad and those brethren couldn't accept the doctrine of the *"blessed Trinity"* because they could not find it in the Bible. That much they had right. Eventually they decided if Jesus wasn't one of three persons of God then he must be *the only person of God*, and that became the Oneness message. Dad spent his life trying to prove that equally non-biblical doctrine. When he was old especially, on radio and in most church services, he included that topic. Joel's mother was a wise woman and tried to encourage him to share more of his vast knowledge of the Bible, but wasn't very successful. Dad Hemphill knew by Scripture that there is **only one God**, and as far as he could tell, it was Jesus, and he wanted the world to know. It was not until 2005 that Joel came to understand from the words of Jesus himself, and his chosen Apostles, that God our Father is the *"only true God,"* and that Jesus our Savior is His supernaturally conceived, virgin-born, sinless, human Son, whose sacrificial death brought us to God *(Matt. 19:17; Mark 12:29-30; John 17:3; Acts 2:22, 33; 3:13, 22; 4:24-30; 7:55-56; 9:20; Rom. 8:34; 16:27; I Cor. 8:6; 11:3; 15:21-28; Eph. 4:6; I Tim. 2:5; I Peter 3:18-22* etc.). Joel has since written four books on this subject. Consider the words of Jesus, the founder of Christianity!

> *"These words spake Jesus, and lifted up his eyes to heaven and said,* **Father***...this is life eternal,* **that they may know thee the only true God,** *and Jesus Christ* [Messiah], *whom thou has sent" (John 17:1-3).*

More of Dad's Teachings

Those who sat under W.T. Hemphill knew how serious he was about serving God. He preached basic Christian practice so simple that even children understood. He taught:

1. **Be careful with your words**. Don't use slang. Mean what you say. Let your word be your bond, and don't say **I bet** or **I swear**!!!
2. **Pay your bills**. If you owe someone a dollar, even if it's in *your* pocket it doesn't belong to you!
3. **Repent**. When you've messed up, repent. That means "an about face." In other words, turn around and go in the right direction.
4. **Do your own praying**. Don't wait on someone else to say a prayer for you.

Pastor W.T. Hemphill

    Call on the Lord yourself. Cry out to Him. Be specific about your needs because the Lord hears and answers prayer.

5. **Pay your tithes**. A tenth of what God has blessed you with goes back to Him and His work. This is a debt that we all owe.

Joel recalls with humor how all of the church youngsters were well aware of Dad's teachings about slang words such as gosh, heck, darn, doggone, etc. and they were daresome to use them. Then someone came up with a clever alternative, a made up adjective that worked just as well. They used it when they were aggravated and they used it when they were exclaiming about something good. That word was "hod-noan," sounding something like "dog-gone." This word became a familiar saying for the youngsters of Bawcomville. If they were frustrated with something they'd say, "that hod-noan thing!" Or if they were surprised or impressed about something they would excitedly exclaim, "hod-noan!!!" Somehow that word made it under Dad's radar, and Joel and his buddies were never called into question about it. Ask anyone who grew up in that village and they will tell you that hod-noan is a famous Bawcomville word.

Dad taught his church to *fast* a meal now and then, especially when you need a prayer answered. He taught everyone to read the Bible for themselves, know what it says! Don't just take someone else's word regarding what *"thus says the word of God."* These are the things that came across Brother Hemphill's pulpit, and he treated people with love and respect. He didn't "beat them over the head" with the things that he believed. He taught them with **kindness** and **led** the people. He loved to quote the apostle Paul when he said; *"Follow me as I follow Christ,"* and he made sure they understood that he meant, *"Follow me* [only] *as I follow Christ."* Because of his love and compassion, Brother Hemphill's flock followed him willingly. They were eager to please him. He was a wise shepherd who knew human nature and understood that the Christian life is a journey and everyone is a work in progress.

Dad Was A Giver
Those close to Pastor Hemphill knew that he used one of his pants pockets to hold **his** money and the other to hold "God's money." If anyone gave him an offering during the day, he immediately deducted the tithes from the gift and put it in the pocket that held God's money. According to him, it wasn't his and it shouldn't go back into building something, i.e. a church for himself. Tithing was for the support of ministry. He believed it was a wonderful plan to bless ministers financially. Since he was not obligated to send his personal tithes to the headquarters of a denomination, he saved it to give to struggling preachers. When visiting ministers came to preach, Dad's tithes, in addition to the love offerings from the saints (and he always gave his people a chance to give), usually was more than enough. Long after Brother Hemphill's passing, ministers who'd preached for him back then said that he blessed them financially more than any other pastor. What a testimony! And no wonder so many great preachers came by the Bawcomville church and blessed that assembly with their ministry. Brother Hemphill was known for his giving. He loved to give and taught his children and his church members to do the same. Many times he'd slip a small roll of money wrapped tightly in a rubber band in the hand of a visiting minister (whether he was

preaching for him or not), and would smile and say "Here's a little ox feed," referring to the Scripture that states:

> *"...Thou shalt not muzzle the ox that treadeth out the corn and the labourer is worthy of his reward" (I Tim. 5:18).*

This great man of God knew the hardships of ministry first hand. He never wanted it said that he received from the Lord in one hand and *closed the other* to his brethren. It would have been unthinkable for him to use a preacher without blessing him financially; it just wasn't done. Because of this, he had the finest ministers to preach in his pulpit. They came often and gave their best because they knew, in return, Brother Hemphill and his assembly would do the same.

Even though Dad was a pioneer and leader of the Pentecostal persuasion he never gloried in being strange. He was sensible, intelligent, and dignified. What he desired most was to please the Lord, and tried to obey the Scriptures to the best of his ability. His services were spiritual but orderly. He knew the definition of *pastor* and he protected his flock from the unnecessary strangeness that is sometimes connected with Pentecostals. If someone got out of order, Dad would gently but firmly steer the service back. His church was made up of his spiritual children, and he had their best interests at heart.

Brother Armstead
It cannot be stated enough how Dad befriended ministers. When Joel was sixteen and had just acquired his driver's license, Dad found out that a minister friend of his who had a moral failure was in California. Brother Armstead was a fallen preacher, and Dad grieved over him, prayed for him, and longed for a chance

to try to restore him. When someone received a postcard from Brother Armstead with nothing more than a San Francisco postmark on the front, that was enough for Dad. He, Joel and Brother Oliver Vallery got in Dad's fifty-one Pontiac and traveled two thousand miles to find (as it were) *a needle-in-a-haystack*. Knowing that he had done carpenter work, Brother Hemphill tracked him down by the carpenters union and found him on his job. When Brother Armstead looked up and saw Dad, his words were, "Brother Hemphill, I knew if anyone came looking for me it would be you." Joel remembers that trip as being the time that he got to drive all he wanted to, and then some.

Sad to say Brother Armstead's entanglement had become so severe that he saw no way out and never returned to his calling. But Dad had the satisfaction of knowing that he had tried to restore him.

Joel's family maintained a low profile and made no apologies for it. They knew what was important, and it was people, not *things*. Joel's dad believed that every person had value and was a potential "diamond in the rough." He treated people with dignity. As long as they were trying to do right, he kept on working with them. It didn't matter how many times they messed up; Dad had hopes that they would eventually get their footing. Many did and became pillars in the church. Even though he was a carpenter by trade, he wasn't into building earthly edifices. It took very little to satisfy him along those lines. He put his time, money and efforts into building people, and he was a hurting person's friend. Brother Hemphill loved the Lord, and God honored his faith and devotion with a thriving church and successful ministry.

Joel's Dad passed away in February of 1981, at the age of eighty-eight. But Brother W.T. Hemphill still lives on in the hearts of those who knew him; yet with his passing, something is gone that can never be replaced, something noble and good. Brother Hemphill's life was a landmark that others could sight by. He was consistent, never wavering from who he was or what he was about, and we know where he is today. He is with Jesus in the bosom of the Father.

> *"...the only begotten Son, who is in the bosom of the Father" (John 1:18).*

Joel had a great relationship with his dad and didn't chafe over the restrictions that he put on him. When Joel wanted permission to go somewhere or do something a little questionable for a pastor's son, he would say, "Dad, the other boys are doing it." Then Dad would say, "Son, others may but you cannot."

The world is a better place because W.T. Hemphill passed through it. He filled his space in time serving God and his fellowman, and great is his reward. But we who remain can't have our headlights on the rear. This is another era. We must look ahead for the wonderful promises of Jesus our Savior who said:

> *"...**He** that believeth on me, the works that I do shall **he** do also; and **greater** works than these shall **he** do, **because I go unto my Father**" (John 14:12).*

We as followers of Christ, need to try and find out why this promise is not being fulfilled in the measure that it should be. What are we needing to learn that we don't already know, to bring this about? The church has had some glory days in the past, but according to the Bible, the best is yet to come! God spoke a promise through the prophet Joel, quoted by Peter in Acts chapter two:

> *"...I will pour out my Spirit upon all flesh; and your sons and your daughters shall prophesy, your old men shall dream dreams, your young men shall see visions: and, also, upon the servants and upon the handmaids in those days will I pour out my Spirit" (Acts 2:17-18).*

We, as the church of the living God, are challenged to find some answers. The church has never stopped with just one enlightenment, just as it didn't stop with Martin Luther, the Wesley brothers, Azusa Street, and the Great Awakening. For reasons that we cannot explain, God has chosen to shine the light on His Word little by little, just as he told Israel: *"By little and little I will drive them out from before thee, until thou be increased, and inherit the land" (Exodus 23:30).* This isn't the time to sit back and say, "We have it all; there is no more truth to be had." Just before his ascension Jesus promised:

> *"But when the comforter is come, whom I will send unto you **from the Father**, even the spirit of truth, **who proceedeth from the Father**, he shall testify of me..." (John 15:26).*

> *"Nevertheless, when he, the spirit of truth, is come, **he will guide you into all truth,...and he will show you things to come**" (John 16:13).*

Dad walked in all of the understanding that he was given for his day. He did it with a single-minded determination and zeal. But there is more! The big question that we must find the answer to is "Why has the church lost its New Testament power?" The next question is "What must we do to get it back?" For those of us who are not satisfied with second best and want a real move of God, we must seek Him for the answers to those all important questions, and I firmly believe **the answer is on the way!**

> *"I want you to be wise about what is good, but innocent in what is evil. And **God**, our source of peace, will soon crush Satan under your feet. To the **only God**, who alone is all-wise, be the glory **through** Jesus Christ forever! Amen (Rom. 16:19, 27; Today's English Version).*

Chapter Seven

Great-Grandfather Tilman

Great-Grandfather Tilman

*A*t the end of the day, when evening shadows began to fall, pleasant sounds of music drifted out of the open windows of the plantation house and floated on the wings of a soft summer breeze. Martha was playing her piano and the rhythmic tunes wafted past the cape jasmine and lilac bushes, and out through the loose-hanging moss on the live oak trees.

The year was 1858. Joel's great grandmother Martha had just recently become the wife of Tilman Hemphill, after the untimely death of his first wife, Eliza. Eliza was Martha's younger sister who had died the year before at the tender age of twenty-seven, leaving behind several small children. Both women were school teachers and skilled musicians. In fact it seemed that the entire Hemphill family, including the children, was musically inclined and played various instruments. On a clear night, if the wind was right, melodious tunes from the grand piano, along with voices raised in song, could be heard in neighboring households, including the shanties on their property where weary slaves were resting from their labors.

Joel's great-grandfather Tilman was a medical doctor as well as a successful business man. He owned a general store, a thriving sawmill and lumber company, plus the 2000 acre plantation where he and his family lived. He also had many slaves to work his fields and do the household chores.

One Hundred Years Later....
On rare occasions something happens to bridge the gap between the past and the present, something that gives us a glimpse of

days gone by. One such occurrence took place on March 15, 1957 when Joel's dad was in the office of the Ouachita Parish Clerk of Court, searching the records in connection with some property that he owned. He was looking though the index book and found the name *Tilman Hemphill*. He knew that he had never transacted business in that name. He always used his full name *William Tilman*, or his initials, W.T., Hemphill. His curiosity being aroused, he searched further, and the index book led him to the book of deeds. When he opened it, he was surprised to find a link to a man that he never knew, his grandfather. His discovery was so significant that it made the front page of *The Ouachita Citizen* newspaper. The heading was in bold block letters; and the article followed.

"Old Deed Shows Grandfather Of Local Minister Paid $2,500 For Four Negro Salves - Mother and Three Children." The article read:

"The deed was dated October 25, 1858 and was written in easily legible longhand. The slaves, bought from Henry H. Slaughter and Joseph P. Crosley, were listed as: 'Sara, a woman aged about thirty years, and her three children, Tarlton, a boy aged eight years; Aron, a boy aged about six years; and Melinda, a girl, about three years, and slaves for life...' The deed was just as carefully and legally written as it would have been for the sale of real estate. It shows that Hemphill (Tilman), who lived in Bienville parish, appointed A.C. McKenn of Ouachita parish as his agent in the transaction.

> *While Rev. Hemphill was in the citizen's office he looked over a copy of an old book of historical sketches of early citizens living in eighteen northwest Louisiana parishes and which was published in 1890. The book showed that Tilman Hemphill owned a total of fifteen slaves in 1860 and that he was a captain in a Bienville parish Confederate Company."*

When Dad Hemphill made this startling discovery about his grandfather Tilman, he decided to make a trip to his own place of birth in Bienville parish. Maybe he could find more answers to the questions that crowded his mind about this mysterious man. Simsboro somehow held an important key to Brother Hemphill's family lineage. He was born there in 1892, and his father Tilman Beauregard was born there in 1861. Now he had found evidence that his grandfather Tilman, whom he or his dad hardly knew anything about, had lived there in opulence.

When Joel's dad and mom arrived in Simsboro, they stopped at an old grocery store, and after asking a few questions, someone directed them to an elderly couple who lived close by. They were in their nineties, and both were small children when great-grandfather Tilman was still around. Brother Hemphill felt that God had directed him to them because the aged lady's memory was sharp and she enjoyed talking and reminiscing about her childhood. She described the big Hemphill plantation house that she had played near when she was a little girl. Her eyes lit up when she talked about the music that came from the piano that was by the window in the living room. She also told Dad about things that he later found on record in the courthouse, such as the early death of Marcus, one of Tilman's sons. The old lady remembered her mother going there and helping out by sitting with him while he was sick. She also recalled the tragedy many years later when a fire burned the big house to the ground.

After talking to that couple, Dad set out to find where his grandfather had lived and had raised his family. Following their directions, he and Mom eventually came upon the old homeplace. What had once been fields had grown into a forest so it wasn't an easy task. But the old chimney was still standing, and Dad was moved to find tangible evidence of his grandfather's existence. He also found the well that he had heard about. But the greatest find was when he stumbled upon the family graveyard where Eliza and Tilman were buried, and it moved him to tears. The graves were hardly recognizable. They were sunken in and all grown up, but the markers were still legible. When he found that, Brother Hemphill grieved over the grandfather that he had never known. Here was tangible proof of his ancestor, his flesh and blood forebear who lived and died on that very spot in days gone by.

When Joel heard about the deserted grave site of great-grandfather Tilman he was also touched, and in recent years went back with a big marble headstone and placed it on his grave.

Following their find, Joel's parents were even more interested to learn about Dad's ancestry. His family that had lived so long ago he now saw as real people with talents and abilities that had gained them renown. But the more he learned about them, it was easy to see that their riches didn't guarantee their happiness or insulate them from tragedy.

Great-Grandfather Tilman

From Brother Hemphill's youth he had not been totally in the dark about his grandfather Tilman. But all the information that he had to go on was what his father T.B. knew and had passed along to the family, and that wasn't much. They knew that shortly after Tilman's marriage to Martha, she gave birth to a son. He named the boy *Tilman Beauregard*, giving him his own name along with the name of his honored Confederate general, P.T. Beauregard. Then six weeks later, Tilman died, leaving behind his family to be divided and his possessions to be squandered.

Brother Hemphill's father, Tilman Beauregard, never knew of his lost inheritance. He died an older man, never having known how wealthy his father, Tilman, had been when he passed away. But Dad Hemphill uncovered many shocking truths when he began to search the records. He found where the courts had frozen his grandfather Tilman's assets and put a large portion of his money in escrow to be divided among the children of his two wives, Eliza and Martha, when they came of age. As the picture began to materialize, it became easy to read between the lines. For instance, it must have been hard for Martha not to have access to the bulk of Tilman's wealth. This was evident because soon after his demise, she took her children and belongings and went to live with her own family in Greeneville, Texas. It could not have been easy for her to leave friends and familiar surroundings. It seems likely that she would not have done so if she had been independently wealthy.

Tilman Beauregard was just a baby when she took him and left for Texas. He had no memory of his place of birth or his father, and Martha told him only what she wanted him to know. She died when T.B. was fifteen, and on her death-bed made him vow that he would never go back and dig into the past, saying that it would only cause trouble, and he never did. By the time Martha passed away, all of her money was gone and T.B. was left in poverty. He was then forced to stay in Texas with Martha's brother and suffered ill-treatment and beatings at the hand of this uncle. Then late one night after his sixteenth birthday, he left and headed straight for Simsboro, the place that his mother often talked about, the place of his birth.

Tilman Beauregard adored his mother Martha. To him she was the perfect saint, and he carried that love and respect for her to his grave. Memories from the past often stirred in Dad Hemphill of his own precious dad singing *"My Angel Mother's Grave"* and weeping over Martha. T.B. cherished her memory all the days of his life. Therefore he did as he had promised her: he never delved into the past. If he had, he would have found some ugly skeletons in her closet. He would have found that his two older brothers, William and Marcus, whom he knew as half brothers, were really his full brothers born to Tilman and Martha out of wedlock. The fact is that Tilman and Martha already had those two sons when he chose to wed her younger sister Eliza. It was Eliza that he gave his name to, and the honored position of queen of his elegant plantation home. Martha was a kept woman and lived on the same property down the road in a small bungalow with her and Tilman's children.

T.B. would have found all of this as a matter of record, had he searched. He would have also found his mother and father's marriage license dated just a few months before he was born. Tilman Beauregard would not have had to search very far until he discovered that he was the only one of the three brothers who was born within the bonds of matrimony, and that at Tilman's

Great-Grandfather Tilman

request the two older boys had been declared his rightful heirs by an act of the Louisiana legislature.

Oblivious to all the above, young T.B. went on with life, working with his hands wherever he could, often only for room and board. Ironically, when he landed in Simsboro and worked as a common laborer cutting timber, it was on the very land that had once belonged to his father. Unknown to him, the lumber company and sawmill for which he worked had more than likely been his father's also. These are things that Martha had kept from her youngest son, simply because she didn't want him to know about her sordid past.

The God Factor
In 1883 Tilman Beauregard met and married a school teacher by the name of Willie Anna Alice Howard, who was a graduate of Clinton Women's College in Clinton, Mississippi. This kind of education for women was fairly uncommon in the 1800's. The couple resided in Simsboro and went on to have six children, three boys and three girls, William Tilman, Joel's dad, being their oldest son. T.B. and Willie Anna then moved their family to Pollock, Louisiana some eighty miles south of Simsboro. There they farmed and eked out a sparse living. They were hard working, salt-of-the-earth type people but not especially religious. This Hemphill family was not spoiled by wealth and the worldly attractions that come with it. Joel's dad looked back to his youth and saw the sovereign hand of God at work in his behalf. He knew that making a living had not been easy for his parents, and they sometimes were short of food, but he was glad that they weren't wealthy. If they had been, Dad wasn't so sure that he would have felt a need for God. The God factor is the most important part of the equation of how our lives turn out.

Our view of God is the greatest influence upon humanity and lies at the core of who we are. W.T. Hemphill found that out and later thanked God for his meager up-bringing.

When W.T. was ten years old an elderly Methodist minister came to Pollock to preach a revival meeting, and he and his family attended those services. That is where his parents were saved, as were W.T. and other members of the family. They became dedicated "Holiness Methodists." About two years after Dad Hemphill gave his heart to the Lord, he felt his call into the ministry. From the time William Tilman was born, T.B. had referred to his eldest son as "doctor." He had dreams of Dad becoming a medical doctor like his father Tilman. He had kept great-grandfather Tilman's doctor bag and instruments, given to him by Martha, and preserved it though the years with great pride. After W.T. Hemphill's conversion, his dad realized that the hand of God was upon him, and relinquished his plans for W.T.'s life, glad for him to answer a higher calling. His words were, "Son, you know that I've always planned for you to be a medical doctor. But now I've decided that I would like for you to become a Holiness preacher and go to Texas and preach the gospel to my mother's family."

W.T. Hemphill was a man who definitely had a call of God on his life. He began preaching at the age of nineteen and was devoted to his call. He was so devoted that, believing that Sunday was the Sabbath, as he traveled here and there to preach, he wouldn't ride on public transportation on Sunday. He thought that if he did, he would be a partaker of the sins of those who were "working on the *Sabbath*." Once, he got off a train with his suitcase and walked for seven miles to do what he thought was right before the Lord. He would tell this with a smile in his later years.

After dad found those forgotten family records he continued the search to learn all that he could about his ancestry. Those searches took him to other Southern States. He found courthouse records in Madison, Georgia, and Raymond, Mississippi, of property such as land, cattle, sheep and money, along with owned slaves that had been passed from generation to generation.

These records go back as far as Joel's great, great, great grandfather, Samuel Hemphill, wed to Elizabeth Bandy, daughter of a revolutionary patriot, Lewis Bandy, who as early as 1810 was bequeathing his earthly goods to his descendants in his last will and testament. Persons with names such as Lucky, Ned, Linus, George, Isaac, John, Caroline, Esther, etc., were deeded along with other properties and passed on to his descendants. However, It was just thirty years earlier that John Adams had introduced the Massachusetts *Bill of Rights*. That bill opens with Article I:

> *"**All men are born free and equal**, and have certain natural, essential, and unalienable rights..."*

It should have been obvious from the beginning that slavery has no place in a free society. But as terrible as it was, it was convenient and lucrative to those who owned them. With slaves there was no end to the wealth they could accumulate. For the next eighty years the Southern states flourished with big plantations and luxurious life-styles. New Orleans led the way with its un-rivaled slave trade, and the wealthy were getting wealthier from the toil, sweat and tears of souls in bondage, and sadly, some of Joel's fore-bearers were involved. The days leading up to the Civil War were the glory days of the South. Egomania was rampant. Many were filled with vanity, conceit, and a haughty, exaggerated self-worth. A great number of those rich slave owners became intoxicated with their riches and acted as though they were above the laws of God, but this was a time-bomb that finally erupted in a full-scale war in 1861.

The *Civil War* pitted friend against friend, and neighbor against neighbor. It separated families and ultimately became a *"war among brethren."* Abraham Lincoln, the great emancipator, called for a *"re-birth"* of this great nation. He grieved over the rivers of American blood that was spilled by our own hand and desperately cried out, *"I'm drowning in blood!"*

Great-grandfather Tilman was disposed to join the fight, along with multiplied thousands of proud Southerners, to preserve his honor and grandiose lifestyle. He became a captain in a Bienville parish confederate company and served under the Louisiana French General, P.T. Beauregard. Tilman died in the early part of the war by natural causes and never knew that the bitter fight would drag on until his beloved South lay in ruins and the ill-gotten gain was spent for naught. The confederates were strong and willful, and the outcome hung in the balance. The South exhausted every ounce of strength and finances it could muster, but it was actually lost for them before the first shot was fired, the reason being, they were fighting for ***bondage***, not freedom!

Slavery is a blight on the pages of our history, but some good did come out of all that suffering. People were brought to the new world that would never have made it otherwise, and heard the gospel of Jesus Christ that they would never have heard in their distant land of spiritual darkness. This nation was settled and developed under very harsh conditions. Our forefathers, slaves and free, fought sickness, disease, starvation, hostile Indians etc. Death was a constant companion to the early settlers. We, their posterity, are now enjoying the fruits of their hard labors. Thanks to them, we can call ourselves the citizens of the most blessed nation under the sun.

It is a must to know history. We learn from it, and then go forward. Every American needs to look ahead, *"With malice toward none, with charity for all..." (Abraham Lincoln; Second Inaugural Address; March 4, 1865)*. Each of us is responsible for **our** actions, and not for those of our ancestors.

When we think of slavery we cannot overlook the Jewish people. They are the greatest examples of those who have endured. They came out of 400 years of bondage in Egypt and yet they rose above it. Through anti-Semitism, there has never been a race as persecuted and looked down on and treated as less than human as they. World War II annihilated about half of the Jewish people on this planet. In fact it was an attempt to stamp out the entire race. At the beginning of World War II, there were 13 million Jews scattered throughout the nations of the world in what is called the *Diaspora* or dispersion. By the end of the war, there were only approximately seven million left. Their number has just now gotten back to where it was before the Holocaust. That is a terrible blow to a race of people. But they outnumber all others in Nobel Prizes and scientific discoveries. Remember, Albert Einstein, Werner Van Braun, and Albert Schweitzer were **Jews**. With this in mind, none of us should allow the attitude of others, past or present, to define for us who we are.

The apostle John kept reminding his readers who they were after they became Christians and his words still apply.

> *"Behold what manner of love the Father hath bestowed upon us, that we should be called the **sons of God**...Beloved, now are we the children of God..." (I John 3:1-2).*

Paul told the Greeks on Mars Hill that through Christ, *"we are the **offspring** of God..." (Acts 17:29).*

Joel's great-grandfather Tilman is a part of this nation's past, who fought for a cause and system that could not continue. But without him, including all of his shortcomings, we Hemphills wouldn't be here. And because he was, now today we are.

What Happened To The Wealth?

In 1957-58 the question as to what happened to great grandfather Tilman's fortune was discovered by Dad Hemphill long after his own father's demise. The records show proof of embezzlement under the pretense of large expense accounts for Eliza's children. The money in escrow was eventually squandered through unethical practices by those who could gain access. It is also likely that Tilman's vast holdings were seized for taxes by the government, taking into account that Confederate currency lost its value, and the slaves were set free when the South lost the war.

> *".....For riches certainly make themselves wings; they fly away like an eagle toward heaven" (Proverbs 23:5).*

Chapter Eight

Lenwil School

Lenwil School

A hush came over the class and every eye turned in Joel's direction when Mrs. Lomax called his name and said in her most demanding tone, "Joel, you are a disturbing factor in this classroom, and I am about to take drastic measures!" The embarrassment of being singled out caused his cheeks to burn and made him want to slide down in his desk and just keep on going, right through the cracks in the floor.

Joel's second grade teacher was a large, stern lady who had never had children of her own. Therefore she expected her rules to be obeyed without question and was unyielding in her demands for orderly conduct. Joel had been caught playing around in class and not paying attention. That was a big no-no to Mrs. Lomax. He had been the object of her displeasure before and wasn't looking forward to the outcome this time. A few weeks back, he and Roger Parrot were whispering and giggling when they looked up and found Mrs. Lomax standing over them with a 12-inch ruler in her hand. Then in her uncompromising manner, she sternly ordered their punishment. "I want each of you to take this ruler and hit yourself on the knuckles, and if you don't do it hard enough I'll do it for you." Her's was the voice of strict authority and Joel took it seriously. With the ruler in his right hand and the edge aimed at his knuckles, he came down hard on his left hand with a "whack." Then Roger took the ruler and hit his hand with little more than a tap. Mrs. Lomax seemed to be satisfied and went back to her desk, but really she was concerned about Joel's hand. In a few minutes she came back to check on him. When she saw that his knuckles had begun to swell, she assumed a sweet voice (which was totally out of character for her) and said softly, "Joel, I didn't mean for you to hit it *that* hard." That aggravated Joel. He was thinking; *"How could I know how hard she meant!?"*

Bawcomville's elementary school was a large frame structure with several smaller buildings adjoining it, all connected by sidewalks. The floor was made of narrow pine boards with occasional knotholes big enough to see the ground through. A janitor kept them clean by using a broom and floor sweep, which helped keep the dust down and also filled in some of the cracks.

Every room had a big blackboard or chalkboard on the wall behind the teacher's desk, and every so often, the teacher would assign two students to take the box of chalk erasers out in the yard to beat them against a tree to remove the chalk; it was an honor to be chosen. The smell of chalk mixed with the pungent scent of floor sweep and knotty pine gave the schoolhouse an air of distinction all its own. The students' desks were one-armed chairs with a compartment underneath to store books.

Joel and his friend Raymond entered the first grade together, but it was Raymond's second time around, as he had failed the year before. Lenwil's first graders sang a little song of safety that the teacher taught them as they left the schoolyard at the end of the day. It said, "I will look both ways before I cross the road, etc..." A teacher was assigned daily to see the children across the road safely, and they sang that song as they marched. A few years later Joel's first grade teacher reminded him of that and said with a smile, "Joel I could hear you singing above everyone, knowing in my heart that you were *not* going to do what the song said."

For the first several years of its existence Lenwil School had no indoor plumbing, only an outhouse, and it was a building of much importance. It measured about ten feet by fifteen feet, and had a concrete floor. For the boys, there was a long urine trough on one side and several stalls with concrete stools on the other. This little house was a place of necessity, and sooner or later you saw most everyone there.

Each day at recess, Mrs. Lomax allowed someone to be in charge of the volleyball, and his or her name was written on the chalkboard. It was an honor to be selected for the task, but it was also a responsibility to be taken seriously. One day Joel's little friend, Jerry Wall, was chosen to have custody of the ball. Jerry was smaller than most of the boys his age, a nice looking kid with olive complexion and black hair. He stirred Joel's compassion because he lived alone with his mother, and Joel couldn't imagine being raised without a father. But on this day, Jerry stood tall and walked proudly in his new tennis shoes. He was in charge of the coveted ball, and his name was on the chalkboard for everyone to see.

When the five-minute warning bell sounded, that meant recess was over, so Joel and Jerry made a last minute dash for the outhouse. When Jerry went in bouncing the volleyball on the concrete floor, someone bumped into him and the ball, causing it to careen and land on the stool. The two boys froze in their tracks and held their breath as they watched the ball roll around on top of the toilet seat, then drop down into the hole with a splash. They stood speechless, then turned and looked at each other as if to say, "What do we do now?!" Jerry immediately began to weigh his options and came to a quick decision; he was going after it! There was no doubt; he had rather go down into the toilet hole than face Mrs. Lomax without that ball!

Joel could hardly bear to watch his little friend as he went into the hole until the toilet seat was under his arms, and then dropped his body into that disgusting place. Then with his feet, he began working the ball up within reach. When he finally retrieved it, he was a mess! His clothes were soiled and his new white tennis shoes ruined. They washed the ball off and Joel took it back to class while Jerry left for home. When Joel handed the ball to Mrs. Lomax she asked, "Where's Jerry?" Then Joel told her what had happened and she lowered her voice and said softly, "That darling boy. He didn't have to do that." But both boys knew better.

Mr. Krum
The year that Joel started to school, Daniel entered the sixth grade. The sixth graders looked big to Joel and Raymond, and those older boys told scary tales about Mr. Krum, the principal. They said that he had an electric paddle in the office that he used on kids that misbehaved. Joel had no way of knowing if it was true because he made sure that he never went there. The rumor about the "paddle with holes in it" was verified by some, but there again, Joel didn't get a first-hand look at *it* either.

Mr. Krum, who also taught sixth grade, was a strong disciplinarian and an imposing figure who wore thick glasses. But about the only time Joel ever saw him was at the outhouse. The older boys said that he was a German, and since that was right after World War II, it made him seem more ominous. Mr. Krum's son, Wilbur, was in the same grade with Dan, and he and some of the kids in their class thought he was too hard on his son. Of course Joel and Dan were mostly disciplined by W.T. Hemphill and because of him, they understood mercy and compassion. Dad always gave them a chance to explain themselves before punishment. If there was a reasonable explanation for their actions, the punishment was not administered.

Dad Hemphill and Mr. Krum had a few things in common but handled discipline differently. Both men would not tolerate much foolishness from children. But where Mr. Krum seemed to enjoy making a spectacle out of his child in front of the class, Dad was more discreet. When he caught his children misbehaving in church, he didn't embarrass them by exposing them in front of the congregation. It was a matter between him and them, and that's the way he dealt with it. If you were caught acting up, all he had to do was catch your eye. Then he gave that knowing wink that meant, "You're in trouble." When that happened to Joel, after church he would catch the first ride going toward home, get in bed and pretend to be asleep. He knew his dad was too compassionate to wake him for correction, and he hoped he would forget about it by morning. It worked a few times, not because Dad forgot, but because he was merciful.

There is one occasion that stands out in Joel's memory. It was a time when he was "tried, and found guilty." So there was to be a session including him, Dad, and the razor strap which hung on a nail in the hallway. Joel had never seen Dad sharpen a razor on that strap, but he and the rest of his brothers and sisters had been "sharpened" on it a few times. That day Dad laid him across his knee and Joel tried to get ready for the impact of the strap. He calls it "scrunching up." Joel felt Dad's arm in motion as he raised it in the air. He heard the sound of the leather strap hitting flesh, three or four times, but felt nothing. Then Dad let him up, and raised his own pants leg and showed Joel the red marks on his leg. Tears were streaming down Dad's cheeks, and he said, "Son, this time I took your whipping for you, and I would take them all if it would do you the good." Joel learned about mercy first hand that day, and he left that scene a better person. In his words "The whipping that I didn't get, did me more good than any other."

Mr. Krum was like so many other men in authority, even pastors, who make an example of their own children, demanding perfection. Joel and Daniel were not accustomed to that. Their dad understood that they were just boys, and never forgot he had been one himself. But he also demanded that they respect authority and the house of the Lord.

The Third Grade
In the third grade, Raymond began to fall behind in his studies. He sat in the back of the classroom near the gas space heater just looking for something with which to amuse himself. One day in the dead of winter, the silence of the class was disrupted by a loud yell from Vernon Redman. The classmates were jarred by the sudden outburst, and the teacher asked sharply, "Vernon, what is wrong with you?" "I don't know," he replied, "Something just burned the back of my neck."

Now Vernon sat directly in front of Raymond and was known for his close haircuts. The sight of Vernon's bare neck and prominent ears were ever present with Raymond, and on this particular day he was overcome with temptation. He thought it would be funny to pull a prank on his friend. So he removed the rubber from the eraser of a Number Two pencil, leaving only the metal band. Then he held the pencil behind him and placing it on the heater until the metal was hot, stuck it to the boy's neck. Of course Vernon screamed out in pain and that's when Raymond's fun took a sudden nose-dive.

When the teacher examined Vernon she found a raised, red circle branded on his tender flesh. And there was no doubt who had put it there. Raymond was then sent to the principal's office and expelled from school for two days.

Raymond was a good natured boy who loved to have fun, but it got him into trouble often, and in more ways than one could remember. As it turned out, that prank wasn't very funny - not to Vernon, and certainly not for Raymond. Raymond didn't pass that year, and that was the last time he and Joel were in the same class.

Marbles
One popular source of entertainment for the boys at recess time was marbles. The school yard was just bare, hard dirt, and while the girls played hop-scotch and jumped rope, the boys played marbles. There were two kinds of marble games, "funzies" and "keeps." When they played "funzies," the rule was that when the game was over everyone got to keep his marbles. "Keeps" was a form of gambling where marbles were lost, and it was strictly forbidden by the teachers. However, that didn't stop it; in fact, it hardly slowed it down.

When "keeps" was played, a boy made a row of five or six marbles, placed about two-inches apart, and then drew a line about three-feet from his row of marbles, where the shooters would kneel and shoot. If a shooter hit one of that boy's marbles he got to keep it. But if the shooter missed, he lost *his* marble.

And there was another way that "keeps" was played. A boy would bring a cigar box with a hole in the lid about the size of a half dollar. The box would be placed on the ground. Then the shooter would hold his marble at waist level and try to drop it into the hole. If he missed, he lost his marble, but if it went into the hole, the shooter got his marble back, plus his choice of one in the box. Every boy had his special pretty marble that he called his "toy" that he would only part with in extreme cases. Also there were oversized marbles that were called "log-rollers." "Toys" and "log-rollers" were common terms to boys of Joel's day, and he says, "Just as familiar as your own mother's name." If a boy put a log-roller in his row of marbles, it was sure to get more shots, which meant a greater win. Every boy that knelt down to shoot would be aiming for the *log-roller*. It was a grand prize.

Joel still remembers the pretty marbles of all colors; reds, blues, yellows - and he still recalls with joy the good times that he had on the Lenwil schoolyard while playing those games with his friends.

Anna Gayle and Mrs. Lomax
A couple of years after Joel left Mrs. Lomax's class, she taught his younger sister Anna Gayle, and Gayle was terrified of her. She had never seen anyone use the "drastic measures" (shaking and pulling hair, etc.), that Mrs. Lomax used when she corrected her pupils. Joel says, "In all fairness to her, it had to be a tough job to keep order in school with children who hadn't had much training at home."

Anna Gayle survived being in Mrs. Lomax's class, but when she was entering the fourth grade, on the first day of school, she happened to pass Mrs. Lomax's room and there sat Rita, their younger sister, in her desk crying. She had heard all about Mrs. Lomax and didn't want her for a teacher. Anna Gayle, today as an adult, is one of the sweetest, most compassionate persons you could meet, but back then she was a slight little girl, small for her age, who wore pigtails, and was a spitfire! She even thought she could whip Joel, who was much bigger and older than she, because his nose bled easily. One day when they were tussling, she bumped it, and it began to bleed. From then on, when she got mad at Joel, she'd warn him, "I'll bloody your nose again!" That same little girl had had it with Mrs. Lomax and was ready to take her on if she had to, but she was determined that her little sister was *not* staying in that classroom!

Anna Gayle walked in and took Rita by the hand, then marched down to the principal's office. She stood her ground and said, "I'll call my daddy and he'll come over here if he has to, but my sister is *not* going to be in Mrs. Lomax's room!" Evidently she got her message across because that day Rita was placed in the other second grade, and Mrs. Lomax never knew why. One day, weeks later, she saw Joel and said to him, "I was sure looking forward to having another Hemphill in my class this year. I thought I had Rita, but for some reason she was assigned to the other classroom. I don't know what happened." Today Anna Gayle jokingly tells Rita, "You still owe me for that!"

The Fifth Grade
In Bawcomville it was a common practice for many of the children to go to school barefooted during the warm season. Joel followed suit. One of his most embarrassing moments happened

Can Anything Good Come Out Of Bawcomville?

one day in the fifth grade, when he looked around and realized that he was the only one there without shoes. He said, "It's like I woke up and found that everyone had quit going barefooted but me! I slid my feet as far under my desk as I could, trying to hide them. I could hardly wait to get out of there. Then I went home and made sure that it never happened again!"

When Joel left Lenwil School, he took with him a wealth of knowledge, and not just from books. He had received insight on human nature and social behavior that books can't impart. Joel also held a degree in understanding authority. After his years in elementary school, he never got confused about who was in charge, and that knowledge has served him well all through life. Though he remembers some tough disciplinarians, he never chafed under their strict rules; he just tried his best to obey them and stay away from their wrath. He found out early in life that if you do as you are told, you escape punishment, but if you are determined to "have it your way" as the song says, then you face the "rod of correction."

Those boundaries helped to shape his character into a law abiding citizen, a good employee, and a God-fearing Christian man. To quote Joel, "I owe a debt of gratitude to the fine teachers at Lenwil: not only Mrs. Lomax, but others such as Mrs. O.J. Parker, Jr., Mrs. Marteil Webb, and Jeff Hennesse." They gave him understanding about the rules of life as well as a formal education, and both are essential if one is to succeed.

Chapter Nine

Taking Communion

Taking Communion

*D*an was nervous. He kept trying to calm Joel down while, at the same time, glancing toward the road. He feared that Mom and Dad might drive up at any minute, and if they did, he would be in *serious* trouble!

It was just an ordinary day; nothing much was happening. Dad and Mom had gone to town to make their rounds at the hospital, and Daniel and his teen-aged friends, Edwin Earl and Freddie, were looking for something to do. Then Dan remembered that his Dad kept a jug of homemade communion wine under lock and key in the big barn out back. The sides of the barn were made of wide planks, and the more he thought about it, he was convinced that it would be easy to remove one of the boards, get the jug, uncork it and let everyone have a taste.

It sounded like fun. They each would get a few swigs, put the cork back, replace the board and no one would be the wiser. Only Dan hadn't counted on his little brother getting tipsy! Joel had taken in several big gulps on an empty stomach and started giggling and staggering. When Daniel realized that Joel was getting *soaked*, he got scared. It was time to do something fast! He had the other two boys keep watch on the road while he hurriedly put the wine jug up. Then he nailed the board back with a sigh of relief. The next thing was to get little brother sobered up before their parents came home. Joel remembers the incident well and the fun he was having getting all of that attention. What he can't be sure of is whether he really *was* "tipsy" or if he was just high on the thrill of scaring the older boys. Whichever it was, although he had very little knowledge of how drunk people act, he giggled, staggered, stumbled, and played the role to the fullest.

The boys got away with their actions that day, and in fact for several days, until Dad went to the barn to pour up the communion wine for the night service. When he did, he found that the cork had been left out of the jug, and there was a thick layer of dead moths and candle flies floating on top of the wine. Then it was judgment day for the Hemphill boys! The scripture that says, *"Be sure your sins will find you out"* became a reality.

Brother Hemphill did not condone drinking in any form; however, he did believe that the fermented blood of the grape should be used for communion, and that Jesus did turn the water into *"wine."* But otherwise he was a teetotaler, and knew what the Scripture says about wine and strong drink.

> *"Wine is a mocker, and strong drink is raging, and whosoever is deceived thereby is not wise" (Proverbs 20:1).*
>
> *"Who hath woe? Who hath sorrow? Who hath babblings? Who hath wounds without a cause? Who hath redness of eyes? They that tarry long at the wine; they that go to seek mixed wine. Look not thou upon the wine when it is red, when it giveth its color in the cup, when it moveth itself aright. At the last it biteth like a serpent, and stingeth like an adder" (Proverbs 23:29-32).*

Dad made his own communion wine because someone told him that what you buy at the store has alcohol added, and he wanted to do everything to the letter. He taught his people to leave alcohol in any form alone, because it has a *hook* in it!

One prominent family that they knew didn't heed the biblical warnings. They embraced the idea that you could not, by the Scriptures, condemn the casual drinking of wine. The parents set the example for their children by drinking in the home, never dreaming that they were paving the road to heartache. They had a large family and several of their children's lives were devastated by the effects of alcohol. Ideas have power, a dangerous idea was planted in those children's minds while growing up, and their parents lived to regret it.

Needless to say, Joel, Daniel and their friends were just normal boys with the usual temptations, but they were surrounded by people who loved the Lord and were loyal to the church. These boys were constantly hearing *the Word* and experiencing the presence of the Holy Spirit. At the Bawcomville church, there was no such thing as children being removed from the main services to go off and play ball or waste time. That would have been unthinkable. The youth were right there taking part, singing and clapping their hands. They were free to testify, sing specials, and pray around the altar. Church was for everyone, which included children of all ages. If they had been removed from the sanctuary, they would never have experienced those wonderful services nor heard the powerful singing and those dynamic sermons. All of these things birthed great desire in the hearts of Joel and the young people of the Bawcomville church to live for God.

The Old Fashioned Altar

It was after the close of a revival of several weeks duration when the boys and several young men were stirred up to spend more time in prayer. Daniel, Edwin Earl, Ralph Beebe, Alsey and Raymond Franks, Freddie Salsbury and others, decided to find a good spot in the woods and build an "old fashioned altar." Of course Joel and Raymond were right with them.

The woods were toward town from the Hemphill house, up Schanks Lane and Jones Road, where the levee would later be. But when the boys went looking for a place to build their altar, there was no levee - just woods with a dirt road winding through. They walked through the forest searching for the right spot and came upon an open space. It was a lovely grassy place that they had perhaps seen before while hunting, but never really noticed. The trees were like a gigantic canopy over the clearing, and when they saw it they were delighted. It seemed almost majestic, and they knew that they had found the perfect spot. There were a couple of trees just a few feet apart, between which they nailed wide planks, then steadied these with boards nailed to the sides. Then they brought wood shavings to spread on the ground around it. The boys worked hard to build an altar that would last, motivated by thoughts of a secluded place where they could spend time in prayer. When it was finished, they gathered around and prayed, not just that day, but many times, especially after a good revival. When they gathered they would pray for an hour or so, then sit around and talk about the Lord. It was a wonderful experience for Joel to be with those older boys and men and hear them pray and discuss spiritual things. As they prayed, some would kneel, others would walk around clapping or raising their hands toward heaven, unashamedly crying out to God. Joel and Raymond were right in the middle of it, following suit.

That *old fashioned altar* in the woods became very popular, and many of the men from the church joined in with them; the Clampit boys, the Jones' boys, even young married men like Joel's Sunday school teacher. It's hard to say who all went there to pray. Eventually the group became so large that they migrated to an old abandoned house that was also in the woods, not for away, for shelter in bad weather.

Brother Oliver
Joel's Sunday school teacher, Brother Oliver, was a handsome young man of French descent, who had a burning desire to serve the Lord. And Joel thought a lot of him. When he taught the class, he would read the scriptures and at times weep over them as he expounded the Word. But at one point, when Joel was about nine years old, Brother Oliver became discouraged in his Christian walk and dropped out of church. He drifted away from God and his better self. Joel really missed Brother Oliver and gave him a call one night after a powerful service. He let him know how much he missed him and encouraged him to come back to church. His wife told Joel at the next service how much his call had meant to Oliver and that he had wept after they hung up. She asked Joel to call him again if he felt like it, and he did. Before long, that dear man did come back to church, this time more dedicated than ever. He became rooted in his faith and became a minister, a pastor, and a wonderful man of God. He told Joel later how much he appreciated those calls and how it helped to turn him around and start him back in the right direction.

Can Anything Good Come Out Of Bawcomville?

There is an ebb and flow to the spirit of revival. There are times when you feel that you could conquer the enemy with one hand tied behind your back. Then there are other times when you have to walk by faith and try to keep your head above the water.

Sad to say that when the revival fires at the Bawcomville church grew dim, the *old fashioned altar* had grass growing up around it. It was during times like these that Raymond, remembering the good times they had there, would exclaim, "Hey Joe, let's go down to the *old fashioned altar call."* In his mind the altar was always connected with the *"altar call"* given at the end of service for sinners to repent. Thus when he spoke of the one in the woods, it was always the *"old fashioned altar call."*

We see in this chapter that these Bawcomville boys, like boys and all people everywhere, were confronted with the "wine" of temptation. But they were blessed more than most, in that they were taught that strength and help can be found at an altar of prayer before God.

Joel

Joel's parents
Pastor W.T. and
Beatrice Hemphill

"Sis Bea"

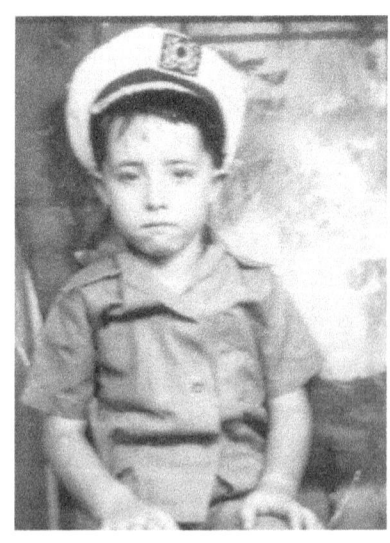

Joel

Joel

Joel and older brother Daniel

Pastor W.T. Hemphill baptizing in LA bayou

Joel's love for horses began early and continues today

In Mexico

Rev. Edward Kelley with wife, Juanita

Evangelists Wilbur and Mildred Milbourn

Dad Hemphill with thirteen of his fourteen children ~ Joel fourth from left

Joel and LaBreeska at sixteen

At seventeen on wedding day

At eighteen

Dinner On Ground

LaBreeska, Joel and firstborn son, Joey

Dad Hemphill and three sons: Daniel, Joel and David

Joel's sisters Anna Gayle and Rita

Jack Smith enjoying the dinner

Bawcomville Church Family ~ 1970's

Bawcomville Church today ~
Joel standing on front steps

JOEL

and

LaBreeska

Mom and Dad Hemphill
Joel, Anna Gayle, Rita, Brenda and David

Joel and LaBreeska
and their children ~
Joey, Trent and Candy

Joel and LaBreeska
Gospel Singers ~ Songwriters

First Hemphill Gospel Band ~ Circa 1920's
Brother W.T. Hemphill with wife Etta (center)

Joel and family singing Gospel music in
Washington D.C. for congressional breakfast

Gospel Singing Family

Joel, LaBreeska, Joey, Trent and Candy

RECEIVING AWARDS

Joel and family receiving Dove Award in 1981, along with producer Jerry Crutchfield and record company executive Mike Cowart

Joel receiving BMI Award for his songwriting from publisher Bill Traylor

MORE AWARDS

A special Alumni award from West Monroe High School for life accomplishments

Joel in front of his bronze plaque commerating his induction into the Southern Music Hall of Fame

Interesting Places and Activities

Scotland on the North Sea

In Hawaii at an old abandoned sugar cane mill

Blowing shofar in Israel

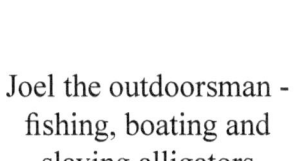

Joel the outdoorsman - fishing, boating and slaying alligators

Thanks to "Old Burr Head", Joel still enjoys his donkeys!

50th Wedding Anniversary

Joel Hemphill,
The boy from Bawcomville

Chapter Ten

Hunting

Hunting

"Did you get anything?"

Daniel had just stepped off the school bus, and seeing his little brother standing in the pasture with his 4-10 shot gun, called out to him.

"I shot a bird but I can't find him" was Joel's reply as the old yellow school bus lumbered on down Jonesboro Road.

Joel had just misrepresented the truth to his big brother. He *had* been shooting at birds but had seen none fall; therefore he wasn't looking for a dead one. Dan, who was seven years older than he, was an avid hunter and a pretty good marksman. Joel looked up to his older brother and hated to tell him that he hadn't hit his target. By now Daniel's interest was aroused, and he decided to help his brother find his lost game. To Joel's dismay, Dan started coming toward him, asking probing questions.

"Where was the bird when you shot him?" Joel responded by lamely pointing at a big tree in the direction that he had shot. By now he was feeling very uncomfortable and guilty about the charade. He hadn't meant to lie; it just happened, and now all he could do was play it out. Anyway there was so much underbrush and dead leaves, Joel figured you could lose a dead squirrel or even a rabbit in it, so there was no need to worry about being found out. When Daniel got to the tree that Joel had directed him to, he stooped down and searched around in the leaves. Then to Joel's astonishment he came up with a dead bird! He said, "Hey! I found him!" Daniel held the prize in the air and flashed a big grin of approval. To Dan this was conformation that his little brother was going to be a good hunter like himself. Joel stood watching in disbelief, but as it turned out, he was the only one surprised. When the two brothers walked across the pasture that day, headed for home, both were happy. Daniel was happy that Joel was already a sure-shot, and Joel was happy that his lie wasn't *really* a lie after all. Dan never knew the difference.

Joel was seven when he got his first gun, but children, especially the boys, raised in Louisiana, (sportsman's paradise) are trained in gun safety at an early age. They hunted squirrels, rabbits, birds, etc. which were in abundance and there for the taking. Joel was taught not to take a life just for sport. A life counted for something. If you killed an animal, then you dressed it (or undressed it) for the skillet. Even if you caught a fish, you were responsible not to waste it. This is the code of ethics that sportsmen should live by.

> *"For every creature of God is good, and nothing is to be refused, if it be received with thanksgiving: For it is sanctified by the word of God and prayer"* *(I Tim. 4:4-5).*

After the bird incident, Dan decided to take Joel with him on little hunting trips. For his big brother to do that was exciting to Joel and made him feel important. Late one afternoon, the two of them were on a hunt deep in the woods when Dan stopped suddenly. He stuck his nose in the air and started sniffing like a bloodhound, then lowered his voice and whispered, "I smell a mink." Joel's blood pressure started rising. This was big stuff! They had hunted for quite a while and had nothing to show for it. Now a mink!? Then Daniel spied a hole at the base of a hollow tree and kept following his nose. "He's in that hole" he said. "We've got to smoke him out." At this point, Dan wasn't just smelling mink, he was smelling money. At fifteen he was "in the know" about hides and such, and mink pelts were selling for $25.00 a piece! This was an opportunity that he couldn't pass up. But they had nothing to smoke the mink out with, so Dan decided to run back to the house for matches and newspaper. Joel was to stay behind and guard the hole in case the mink tried to escape. Joel trained his shotgun on the tree and assured his brother that the mink had better not show himself; if he did "he'd make a sifter out of his hide." With that, Dan took off for home.

It was late in the day and soon the sun started going down behind the trees. When that happened, Joel's interest began to shift. The mink in the hole lost its importance as he became more aware of his shadowy surroundings. Before long he found himself in total darkness, and stars could be seen though the trees.

The nocturnal creatures began to stir and the forest became alive with night sounds. There were rustling leaves, a screeching owl, a snapping branch, along with grotesque shadows of the unknown that seemed to be closing in on him. All these things set Joel's imagination to racing, and *he* jumped up and started racing too. He had no idea where he was; he'd left that up to his brother. Now he was by himself in the woods in absolute terror and didn't know which way to go. Joel says, "Whenever I got lost it seemed the best thing to do was to start running and crying. It didn't help all that much, but it's the first thing that came to mind; and at least you are doing something."

Can Anything Good Come Out Of Bawcomville?

The brothers had wandered deep into the woods, and it took Daniel much longer to go home and come back than he'd figured. When Dan finally got to the area where he left Joel, he had to chase him down to catch him. He said he could hear him a long way off, running in circles, crying and praying.

Now here's the big question. Was there really a mink in that hole? Of course there was! A nice big one, lodged in the imaginations of two daring young men on safari in the backwoods of Bawcomville!

One day Dan and his two side-kicks, Edwin Earl and Freddie (better known as Peabody), were about to go on a hunt. When Joel discovered that his big brother was going hunting without him, he set in to go along. Joel promised that he'd keep up and wouldn't be any trouble. Dan decided to take him with them. The other two finally gave in and off they went to the woods.

It wasn't easy for a seven-year-old to keep up with teenage boys, but he did. They trudged through underbrush and briers, forged streams and climbed fences with Joel right behind them. One of the older boys, feeling sorry for the little guy, turned to check on him. Then he stopped stone cold. When he looked down at Joel's gun he saw the hammer cocked and ready to fire! When he discovered that, he let out a yell to the others, "Joel has been following us all this time with his gun cocked and loaded!" The boys stopped in their tracks and turned their full attention in his direction. Sure enough, there it was for all to see. At that moment Joel was as guilty as the cat who ate the canary and suddenly became very unpopular. He was public enemy number one, and Daniel was public enemy number two because he was *kin* to him! Edwin Earl and Peabody wanted nothing to do with

Hunting

either one of the Hemphill boys for the remainder of the day, and they turned and left in a huff while Joel and Dan stood watching. Needless to say, that put an end to Joel's hunting excursions with the older boys. From then on, it was he and Raymond Heard, or Alvin and Garland Jones, and their trusty 4-10's.

The Thorn
Joel and Raymond were hunting in the woods one day when Joel stepped on a thorn. He had his rubber boots on to protect him from the dangers of the wild such as snake bites or thorns, and it had always worked. But this thorn was big and sharp and went right through Joel's boot into his foot, then broke off. There was no way to get hold of it to pull it out and no way that Joel could walk with the thorn stuck in his foot. Every move caused excruciating pain. When the boot moved, the thorn would gouge deeper into the flesh. All Joel could do then was sit down on the ground in pain while Raymond went home for help. When Raymond reached his dad, he couldn't make him understand the seriousness of the problem. Brother Heard just waved him aside and assured Raymond that Joel would be fine; he had other things to do. So Raymond believing his dad, forgot his buddy and left him in the woods to fend for himself. When Joel realized that Raymond wasn't coming back with help, he started crying and praying. "Oh Lord help me!" he cried, while calling on the name of Jesus. "Help me Lord!" The more he prayed the louder he got.

Now it just so happened that old Mr. Moore, known to all as "Pop," had decided to take his grandson for a walk in the woods. It was late in the day, but he just had a sudden urge to take a stroll. The two walked along, but stopped when they heard Joel crying and praying. When Pop Moore got to Joel, he spoke comforting words as he took out his pocket knife, knelt down, slit the boot and removed the thorn. Joel thanked him and took off for home. Years later when Joel was in his teens and worked at Owens store, Pop Moore was a regular customer. Occasionally, with a twinkle in his eye, he would remind Joel of the day he found him in the woods with a thorn in his foot. He would smile and say, *"Son you were crying and praying and really telling the news!"*

Joel knew in his heart, and so did Pop, that his prayers had been answered. He knew it then, and he knows it now. It is one of his little monuments of faith, tucked away in his heart, of the time that the Lord heard him and came to his rescue by causing an old gentleman to decide to take his grandson for a stroll in the woods, right when and where he was stranded!

Chapter Eleven

They Saw It On The Radio

They Saw It On The Radio

The Hemphill family's main entertainment and connection to the outside world was a large Stuart-Warner radio that sat on a table in the living room. The sound waves would flow in and out, depending on the weather between them and some faraway place. XEG and XERF were the preaching stations and Mom and Dad's favorites. Those high wattage transmitters that beamed from across the border down in old Mexico came in loud and clear, taking you inside exciting revival meetings where there was an abundance of preaching and singing. The organs, pianos, guitars, and tambourines, would be beating out happy Gospel music and made you feel as if you were sitting there in the congregation.

Joel's parents had a smaller radio in their bedroom, and they would often lie in bed at night and enjoy those programs. One night Dad was listening to a preacher who had a healing ministry. He invited those who needed healing to lay their hand on the radio as he prayed for the sick "out in radio land." Dad Hemphill was a strong man who wasn't afraid of strenuous physical labor and had developed a hernia over the years. It was a bother to him, and every day before he dressed he had to strap a truss (a padded device of support) around his mid-section to hold the bulge in place. As the preacher prayed that night, Dad laid his hand on the radio and by faith in God, received healing for that hernia. He said he felt it "zip up." From then on, Dad never had a need for the truss.

The Bible
The radio was also a great place to advertise and promote the sale of diverse items. The Hemphills took advantage of some of

the great deals offered. First there was Joel's Bible. Late one night Dad Hemphill noticed that Joel's light was still burning. When he went in to turn it off, he found his eight-year-old son deeply engrossed in reading the Scripture. A bare light bulb hung from the ceiling of Joel's bedroom, which wasn't much to read by but it was enough. After a few more incidents like that one, Dad and Mom decided it was time for Joel to have a Bible of his own. They ordered one from an XEG radio preacher and had his name engraved in gold letters on the front. Joel cherished that Bible and still has it today.

Joel was just a boy when he first discovered the heroes of faith in the Old Testament. His favorite books were Judges, Samuel and First and Second Kings. He would read into the night, fascinated with the feats of the great prophets, judges, and rulers of Israel. He loved to read of the miracles they performed, as when Elisha made the ax head swim out of the Jordan River when one of the young prophets was felling a tree and lost it. He was intrigued by the accounts of Elijah: how he prayed that it wouldn't rain because of Israel's sins and for three and one-half years there was drought. Then he prayed again and it rained. This story of the contest on Mt. Carmel when Elijah and the false prophets met to see who *God is,* moved Joel greatly. He loved it when God proved Himself to Israel that day by sending fire down out of heaven and burning up the sacrifice that Elijah had properly prepared. The fire not only consumed the sacrifice but the wood that was soaked with twelve barrels of water, the stones of the altar, and the dust, and even licked up the water that was standing in the trench. Then Elijah slew the four-hundred false prophets of Baal who were causing Israel to sin. But most of all Joel loved reading about King David and how

God gave him multiplied victories over his enemies. This great leader of Israel was his favorite hero in the Old Testament.

Through those Bible stories and many more, Joel began to get a glimpse of the Lord God, creator of heaven and earth. God's great power, His faithfulness, and His abundant love for His children began to emerge from the pages of His Holy Word and found lodging in the heart of a very young Joel Hemphill. This knowledge began to grow into a deep respect for God's word, His laws and a reverential fear of His awesome presence. From that time Joel has had an insatiable thirst for the Word of God, and a great love for truth. But he was also a normal mischievous boy who couldn't help but get into trouble from time to time.

The Pilots Suit
There were other things that the Hemphills ordered from radio pitchmen. Since you couldn't actually see the item being offered, with the word pictures that the announcers painted it, was easy to get taken. An example of this was the offer of the government surplus pilot's suits, designed and produced at great expense, to be worn when they flew over the Arctic. This attire that "cost the government hundreds of dollars," was being offered at the "unbelievably low price of $29.95." When the announcer described this piece of clothing, one could visualize fur-lined parkas made of soft, supple leather. Though Louisiana's winters are not that severe, Joel's mother could picture him being kept warm in one of those wonderful suits. It was "an offer of a lifetime," so Mom ordered one for Joel.

There were weeks of anticipation, of watching the mailbox and waiting. Finally the package came. Mom and Joel tore it open and brought out the prize. When they saw it, they just stood there trying to figure it out. It was a quilted nylon jumpsuit with electric wires running all through it like those in an electric blanket. The wires joined and made a cable about three feet long that hung from the back of the suit like a tail, and a strange looking plug was attached to the end. Everyone stood there puzzled, disappointed and amused, trying to make sense of the contraption. They finally realized that the wire was intended to be plugged into an airplane to create heat for the pilot. It was also a rude awakening. They had been "duped!"

Of course the jumpsuit was no good to them or anyone else except a pilot flying over the Arctic, and only then if he had the right sized outlet to plug it into! So they bundled it up and sent it back for their guaranteed refund. You can guess the rest. They never saw the suit nor the money again. That episode gave new meaning to P.T. Barnum's famous saying, *"a sucker is born every minute and two to take him."* But when Mom heard the advertisement on genuine, simulated, diamonds for $19.95, she didn't bite. Number one, jewelry was frowned upon at the Bawcomville church, but that wasn't the only reason. Mom understood the double-talk when the announcer said *"gen-u-wine **simulated** diamonds."* But you can be sure there were plenty of *takers* from that cleverly worded advertisement that padded someone's pockets hundreds of miles away!

The Wish Book
Mail order catalogs were also popular at that time. *Sears and Roebuck* and *Montgomery Ward* were tops on the list. While trying to establish the church at Bawcomville, Dad, Mom, and Daniel painted houses and hung wallpaper to help supplement the family income. The Montgomery Ward store downtown was where Dad bought all of their painting supplies. He developed

such a good rapport with them by being a regular customer - and punctual with his payments - that they gave him ten percent off on all his purchases. They also recommended Brother Hemphill to their customers to install wallpaper and do painting. It's easy to understand why Montgomery Ward became Dad's favorite place to shop. And their mail order catalog, which was called the "wish book" by country folk, held a special place in the Hemphill home. While searching the pages one day, Joel's eyes fell on a pair of lace-up leather boots. The thing that made them irresistible to young Joel was the little pocket on the side of one boot for your hunting knife. He was fascinated by that, and the more he looked at those boots, the more he wanted them. So Mom placed the order and Joel waited impatiently for them to arrive.

When the boots finally came, they were everything that the picture and the advertisement had said, and they fit him perfectly! Joel just loved his new leather boots, but right away someone said, "It's too bad that they're not waterproof." Dad spoke up and said, "That's not a problem. The old timers waterproofed their boots with tallow (fat)." Dad had even done that himself in times past. So the next order of business was to go to Owens store, get some beef fat and put it in a pan, place it on the stove, melt it down, then apply it to the boots. When they finished the process his lovely new boots were a mess! As the tallow dried, it became cracked and smelly. The leather was greasy, splotched, and uneven in color. They looked awful! From then on the boots were absolutely ruined. They were worthless to him and soon became just another lesson in life. Joel decided that tallow might have worked for boots in another century, but it didn't work for him!

Around the same time, Mom decided to order Joel some tennis shoes from the catalog. And once again he began watching for the mailman. Joel had never owned tennis shoes but Daniel had, and he began trying to describe them to him. He built the shoes up by saying they would make a person run faster, jump farther, and climb trees better. Joel could hardly believe what he was hearing, but Dan assured him that they really worked. Joel's imagination began to work also! He thought the shoes must be magic. With that in mind, he could hardly wait for them to arrive. When the package finally came, Joel rushed to put the shoes on. He was excited and didn't know what to expect but was sure he was about to experience something new. When he slipped his feet into the shoes, laced them up and stood, his anticipation was high. He tried running, jumping, and climbing but saw no improvement over what he had experienced *barefooted*. Those tennis shoes weren't magic at all, but they had added a few days of anticipation to the life of a Bawcomville boy!

Chapter Twelve

The 38 Special

The 38 Special

Jack Smith

Where you have ministry as successful as Brother Hemphill's, with a heart as big and compassionate as his, you have all kinds of characters as hangers-on. Jack Smith was one of those characters. He weighed about three hundred pounds, rode a bicycle, and kept plenty of chewing gum and chocolate candy bars in his hip pocket. To look out and see Jack rolling into the yard, dusty and drenched in sweat, was a familiar sight. And he always came bearing gifts. In the summertime, the candy and gum would be soft from the heat and curved to the shape of his posterior.

Jack was generous and enjoyed sharing his treats with the kids. One of his favorite candy bars was chocolate with a marshmallow filling, called a *Bobcat*. Jack called it a *Bob Tat* because he couldn't talk plain. He called a pencil a *pen-staff*, and when he heard irritation in Joel's mother's voice when she had all she could take from him, he'd say with a twinkle in his eye, "Bea-wafus is a fuss-tiwwy," meaning, "Beatrice is a fuss-kitty."

In many ways Jack was like a child; he was also good natured and had a sense of humor. The children enjoyed him and he was around the Hemphill house much of the time in Joel's younger years. Jack couldn't read a word, but he carried his Bible everywhere he went. It was stuffed with papers and bulged so that it had to be held together with a big rubber band. Jack's favorite scripture was Revelation 21:8: *"...all liars shall have their part in the lake which burneth with fire and brimstone...."*

He knew exactly where that scripture was; he had it marked and could turn right to it - the reason being that he would try to get Joel or anyone else to make him a promise. Then he would quote that scripture like this, "Okay Joe, you know what the Bible say: 'all liars have their part in hell fire and *broomfield* '." Then he'd turn to that verse in the Bible and point. It was his way of persuading people to do what he wanted them to do. If he got a promise or even a "maybe," he was going to hold them to it with that scripture.

The Dump Truck
Jack also used his gum and candy bars as a bribe. For instance he'd offer a bent *Hershey* bar to Slim Clampit to get to ride in his dump truck. Slim's dump truck was the only mode of transportation for the kids of Bawcomville to go to the stock car races over in West Monroe. Joel got to go a few times - without his dad's knowledge. On many occasions after church, Slim would load up a group of the youth to go for ice-cream. Or if there was a church function such as a barbeque, or ice-cream supper at the park, a few of the kids would climb into the back of Slim's dump truck and away they would go. Jack was always bargaining with whatever he had to bargain, bribe, or coerce with to be in on the excitement. He was determined to ride in the dump truck with the crowd, even if he had to pull out the Bible and quote his favorite scripture.

Slim's dump truck was a source of pride for him. He was much in demand and very popular because of it. He was also sweet on Urma, one of the pretty girls from the church, but when he showed up to take her on a date in that dump truck she was *not* happy! He couldn't understand her disdain for it. His truck had never seemed out of place in Bawcomville until then. Slim was a nice looking young man. He was tall, about 6'3", and very slender with black wavy hair and a nice smile. He seemed to be a good catch. Joel believed that Slim would have had a better chance at winning Urma's hand if he'd had a car. As young as he was, he could see that it might be hard for her to get romantic in that dusty old dump truck.

It wasn't long before Sister Ruth, an impressive lady evangelist, came to Bawcomville from Southern California for a revival meeting. She was magnificent in the long white flowing robes that she preached in. She was also single and swept into the Bawcomville church like a creature from another planet. When she saw young Slim, she was smitten and set out to win his affections, and did so without much effort. It mattered not that she was a few years older than he, he jumped at the chance to go to faraway places and ride in style. When Slim and Sister Ruth got married, they left for California, and that was the end of Bawcomville's most popular dump truck and the many exciting adventures it provided.

Nelson Johnson
Dad seemed to always be taking in someone who was in need of spiritual guidance, and Nelson Johnson fell into that category. Nelson was a handsome nineteen-year-old, with olive complexion, black wavy hair and a mustache, and was bunking in the little house in their yard. In Joel's younger years, that little house seemed to have someone in it most of the time.

When Nelson came to stay with the Hemphills, he and Dan became fast friends. They were both teenagers and were glad to have each other as companions to hang out with. One warm summer afternoon, Joel was standing in the back yard when

Can Anything Good Come Out Of Bawcomville?

Daniel and Nelson ran past him at break-neck speed. They came tearing around the house, looking as if their lives were in danger. Without a word, the two boys cut through the chicken yard, ran into the outhouse and locked themselves in. Joel was bewildered. He stood gazing toward the privy, trying to understand what was going on, when suddenly Margaret Middlebrook appeared from the same direction waving a loaded 38 caliber pistol. "Joel, is Dan and Nelson in that outhouse?" she asked with fire in her eyes. Joel could see that things were not looking good for his older brother so he answered, "No!"

"Did they come this way?" was her next question. "Yeah, they came running by me but they took off through the pasture," he said as he gestured toward the barn in the opposite direction. Believing Joel, she took off in hot pursuit. As soon as Margaret was out of sight Dan and Nelson came bursting out of the toilet and headed for parts unknown, as fast as they could go. Now Joel's parents were out of town that day for a fellowship meeting. They had left early and wouldn't be home until midnight. It was a common occurrence for young Joel to stay with his fourteen-year-old brother Dan when they had to make such trips, even if they were gone for a couple of days. It was a good set-up since Joel loved being at home. There was so much he could do to occupy his time and plenty of people were always around, other than Dan and himself. Most of the time you could count on Jack Smith being there, or Brother LePrerie who lived in a tent just down the road.

Things usually ran pretty smoothly when Mom and Dad were away, but today the turn of events had taken on a serious nature. Daniel and Nelson Johnson were in trouble, and young Joel was puzzled. What had they done to Margaret to make her so mad?!

The 38 Special

Why would she want to shoot them?! As he was mulling these questions over in his mind, Margaret appeared again - still angry and still waving that loaded 38 pistol! By now she'd figured out that Joel had lied to her. She said, "Joel, I'm going to kill that Nelson Johnson! He promised to marry me; now he's backed out. When I find him I'm going to blow him away!" With that she turned and stormed off in the direction of her home next door. There was no doubt in Joel's mind that she would do what she said if she caught Nelson.

The Middlebrooks, Mrs. Middlebrook and her three daughters, were neighbors who rented from Dad Hemphill. The mother was a short, chubby, easy-going lady who spent much of her time outside working in her flowers. The youngest girl "Pete" was about thirteen at this time and wore glasses. Flora Mae was around fifteen. Both girls were studious and mild mannered. Then there was Margaret! She was the oldest of the three. Joel figured her to be about eighteen, and even though he was just a kid, he considered her to be a woman of the world. One thing; she used language that didn't sound good - and was never heard around the Hemphill house. She also dressed differently than anyone he'd ever seen...in short skirts and black leather boots that came up to her knees.

Margaret wasn't always around. She would disappear for days at a time, and then show up as though nothing had happened. No one ever said why she left home or when she'd be back. She had just recently caused a stir in the community when she came home with a 38 Special that she enjoyed firing in the pasture. The neighbors started complaining. They were afraid that someone was going to get hit by a stray bullet.

Can Anything Good Come Out Of Bawcomville?

Margaret Middlebrook was definitely *not* your average teenager. She was a wild-child, and when Nelson lied about marrying her, he got on her "fighting side." He had stirred up a hornet's nest, and someone was about to get hurt!

Jack Smith was at the Hemphill house the day Margaret came after Nelson with her revolver. When he saw what was happening, he got so upset he ran to the phone and tried to call the law. Milton Coverdale was the sheriff at the time - that much Jack knew. When the operator asked, "Number please?," he was real excited and blurted out, "Operator, I need Co-her-dale! Gimme Co-her-dale!" Sure enough, she connected him with someone at the Sheriff's office because he went on, "Co-her-dale, Margaret's got a gun! She's gonna kill Na-hun at Hemphill's house. Hurry!" In just a short while, a well-worn patrol car came easing by in front of Joel's house like Barney Fife of Mayberry. On the surface all seemed calm and quiet, so they went on.

Shortly after dark, Dan and Nelson came slipping home. They were visibly shaken, dirty and out of breath. Both told Joel they had hidden out at the church the rest of the day. They'd crawled under the platform in fear and trembling and prayed while keeping a watch for Margaret.

In the mid-forties, the church was in its infancy and the building was nothing more than an up-scaled, open-air tabernacle with a sawdust floor. In the winter, the men put paper mill canvas around it to keep the cold out. Then in the summer, they took that down and replaced it with wire fence to keep the cows out. The platform was about two feet from the ground, just high enough for Daniel and Nelson to crawl under for protection as they waited for night to fall and the coast to clear.

Brother and Sister Hemphill came home around midnight of that same day to a quiet and peaceful house. The following morning, before anyone stirred, Nelson felt an urgency to leave the premises for awhile till everything cooled down. He gathered his belongings and without fan-fare, left in search of a safer place to reside, thus ending the saga of the 38 Special.

The Birds and The Bees
After Nelson left, Dad got wind of all the ruckus that had gone on between him and Margaret. He figured it was time to talk to his boys about the birds and the bees, and called Joel and Daniel aside. He seated them on the front-porch swing and looked each one in the eye and asked them individually, "Son have you ever touched a woman?" Now Daniel, at 14, understood what Dad meant, but it was hard for Joel to wrap his seven-year-old mind around that question. Dad went on to warn them not to be misbehaving with girls. First of all it was a sin, and there was a danger in catching unwanted diseases. Also people had been shot by angry fathers for fooling around with their daughters. He was not only trying to put the fear of God in them, but also the fear of a double-barreled shotgun. This was rather heavy stuff for a seven-year-old, but Joel pretty well got the message.

Dad was wise and had much experience with people, so during that time he thought it would be good to gather the men of his church in a back room and give them a lesson in sexual purity and even moderation with their wives. One brother, an old man who probably didn't weigh much over one hundred pounds and had already fathered nine children, was there listening to Dad speak. In a few minutes, someone saw him get up and leave, and as he went out the door they heard him mumbling, "There is no need for me to stay in here; this has nothing in the world to do with me."

As Joel grew older and could understand, Dad taught him more about physical relations. He said, "Son, sex is not just to produce children, but it was given by God for the pleasure of a husband and wife to keep them coming back together." Dad was very modest regarding these matters, especially in his conversation. But he knew that a healthy outlook in that regard was very important to a well-rounded person. Something this important, Dad wanted Joel to hear from him; he didn't just leave it for his boy to figure out for himself. Dad knew that sex is a subject that gets out of balance sometimes with religious people, especially the "super religious."

The account of Dad's talk to Joel and Daniel about the birds and the bees made the rounds in the family. Dad's old-fashioned way of handling things of that nature was amusing to the older children, especially Juanita. Even after he was grown and married, she would occasionally tease Joel by zeroing in on him with a mischievous look in her eye and asking, "Son have you ever touched a woman?"

Joel's older sisters, Verba and Juanita, were bright spots in his life. They loved their little brother and never failed to show it in various ways, even good-natured teasing. Juanita would often tell him that she didn't know if he would ever amount to anything or not because Jack Smith and Raymond Heard had taught him everything he knew. But they were just two among many characters who added their special ingredient to the spice

The 38 Special

of Joel's life. From the cradle up, he was surrounded by people. Many highly educated and gifted men and women of renown sat around their table. Then there were the common folk, hard working, salt-of-the-earth men and women who made up the bulk of the Bawcomville church. Each one was a colorful addition in the patchwork of Joel's world, and in their own way, helped to enrich his life. Even a jilted woman named Margaret with a 38 special revolver!

To Dad Hemphill, whoever God sent his way for a short stay or to become a part of the church, was the raw material that he had been given to do the work to which he was called. He understood that each person belonged to the Lord first; therefore he handled them with love and patience because that's who he was. And he believed with all of his heart that someday he would give an account for each one who came under his influence.

Chapter Thirteen

The Church

The Church

*A*s was said in a previous chapter, other than school, the church and its members were pretty well the extent of Joel's world in those early years. Interesting and colorful characters, too numerous to count, were in and out of the Hemphill home. There were Gospel singers and preachers of all descriptions, and very gifted songwriters and musicians who played the piano, accordion, or guitar and sang with expertise and flare.

Brother Wilbur Milbourn and his pretty auburn-haired wife, Mildred, were some of the church's favorites and held several revivals during Joel's boyhood. Brother Wilbur had an abundance of dark wavy hair and a mouthful of "pearly whites" that glistened as he sang and played the accordion. The church came alive when that classy couple stepped up to the podium and started singing. Their ministry was entertaining, but beyond that, his sermons were energetic, powerful and anointed. And their meetings lasted as high as five to six weeks at a time.

Another memorable minister who came often was Sister Peggy. She was the no-nonsense type who usually worked up a sweat when she preached - and had great results. She was quite an artist with words and could paint a vivid picture of you if you weren't living right. She had the gift of discernment, and often she'd stop in the middle of her sermon - and it would get so quiet that the congregation seemed to stop breathing. Then she'd say in dramatic tones something such as, "People complain, 'My spouse just doesn't understand me.' And somebody here has been *understanding* somebody else's wife." Then she would continue, "Just remember...if they'll run around *with* you, they'll run around *on* you!"

Sister Peggy had many insightful sayings. She'd often say, "I'm just shooting down in the hole. If you get hit, get out of the hole!" Her sermons made folk want to clean up their acts and rid themselves of bad habits. Tobacco was a main target and was strictly taboo in Dad's church. Smoking was preached against and named as sin right along with lying, cheating, drinking and running around. Long before it was medically proven to be destroying people's health, tobacco, in any form, was unacceptable and had no part in an overcoming Christian's life. Even coffee didn't escape Sister Peggy's criticism; because of the caffeine content, she condemned its use as well. One member said to her, "But Sister Peggy, I drink *Sanka* and its ninety-seven percent caffeine free." Her reply was, "Well, you lack three percent lining up!"

At the end of Sister Peggy's sermons, some of the young men would go to the altar and repent, then go to the back door of the church and throw away their cigarettes. Knowing how hard it was to give up the habit, a few of them were said to have watched where they landed, just in case. After the service was over and the Spirit had lifted, you might find one of them out in the dark searching through the weeds for his pack of cigarettes.

There was such a stigma against smoking that the children thought it was mentioned in the Bible. One Wednesday night during youth service, Sister Audrey, the youth leader, was asking various youngsters to quote one of the Ten Commandments. Joel's little brother David, raised his hand and when he was called on said with confidence, "Thou shall not smoke."

When Joel was very young he found out just how frowned upon tobacco was when he and Anna Gayle were caught smoking a pipe. It was the smallest pipe they had ever seen and they were fascinated by it. If it had been the regular size they probably wouldn't have been tempted, but that little pipe was so cute, the temptation to try it out was overpowering. But they had nothing to put in it. They tried some weeds called "rabbit tobacco" but that didn't work very well. Then they thought of the Schanks boys who lived across the road and smoked, so they found six-year-old Donald Ray, their younger brother, and Joel sent him home to snitch cigarette butts from the ashtrays. Donald Ray came back and proudly handed over his plunder, and when they used that up, he was sent back for more. That's when he got caught and "the fat was in the fire!" To Joel and Anna Gayle's dismay, Sister Schanks came charging across the road with Donald Ray in tow. She had him by the arm and his feet were only touching the ground every few steps. When she got to the front yard she started calling out, "Brother Hemphill! Brother Hemphill!" The alarm in her voice brought Dad from the back yard. When she spotted him coming around the side of the house she blurted out, *"Brother Hemphill, there is sin in the camp!"*

Joel was familiar with the Bible story of Achan in the book of Joshua who caused the defeat of Israel at Ai. It tells how Israel had defeated Jericho with a great victory and was warned by God not to take any of the spoils. If they did, it would *"**make the camp of Israel a curse** and trouble it. But Achan saw among the spoils a beautiful Babylonish garment and two hundred shekels of silver and a wedge of gold...**and took them**..."* and buried them in the ground under his tent. After Achan confessed to disobeying the Lord and causing the death of thirty-six men, the people rose up *"and all Israel stoned him with stones..."* *(Joshua 6:18; 7:21-25).*

When Sister Schanks said *"there's sin in the camp,"* Joel understood the gravity of their situation. He also knew that he and Anna Gayle were not going to escape the consequences; they would pay for their actions with sore backsides. And they did!

Brother Duke
Brother Joe Duke was another minister who came often to hold revivals, and kept the audience spellbound. He was an imposing figure behind the pulpit. He stood well over six feet tall and wore very thick, horn-rimmed glasses. When he preached, he intended to put the fear of God in you. And it worked, especially on the younger generation.

At the close of his sermons, Brother Duke was "seeing visions" of black caskets long after they had quit making them. But he got results. When he gave the invitation, people would fill the altar in great numbers. It was in one of his meetings that Joel got saved at the age of ten. One of the most effective things that Brother Duke did was to stretch his long arms straight out in front of him and clap his hands. Then he would say "Bless God, if you don't have the Holy Ghost you'd better have it by Friday!" He never said what would happen on Friday, and the sinners didn't wait around to find out. The altars filled up and sure enough, many "got the Holy Ghost *before* Friday!"

Brother Duke was well known throughout Pentecostal circles for his powerful ministry. There were usually more people saved in his revivals than in most any other, and you could always count on a few outstanding miracles to take place. He was a real man of God with great faith, a little strange, but so were the prophets of old.

Soon after one of Brother Duke's revivals, Joel and Raymond were walking home from school. It was report card day and a sad time for Raymond. He had straight F's written in red, and with every step he took, he was dreading his arrival at home. His parents were devout Christians and faithful members of the church. Brother Heard was a successful oil driller and Sister Heard was a good homemaker and president of the P.T.A. But for some reason, Raymond was a slow learner. His parents did everything within their power to help him. Many mornings when Joel came by Raymond's house on the way to school, Sister Heard would be drilling him right up to the last minute on his spelling, arithmetic, etc., but nothing was working. Raymond's education was an on-going battle that never seemed to end, and he was well aware of how exasperated his parents were with him. Raymond also knew that his dad had decided that he just wasn't applying himself and had warned him what would happen if he ever brought home another bad report card.

That's the way things stood that day when the boys were on the way home from school. What Raymond needed was a miracle! The closer he got to home, the more desperate he became. Then he stopped, looked at Joel and solemnly said, "Joe, I wish Brother Duke was here. He could pray these F's off of my report card!"

Imon Ursery
One of the most gifted and interesting women that came to preach at the Bawcomville church was Imon Ursery. She was dynamite in a small package. Her ministry spanned several

decades and reached into the seventies. Sister Ursery, as everyone called her, was a petite lady minister and poet with an abundance of strikingly beautiful auburn hair. She spoke with a soft voice as she preached up and down the aisles. You had to lean-in in order to hear her, but her sermons were delivered with great energy and passion. When she broached a subject, it was evident that she had done her homework. She knew what she was talking about and was going to tell you something that you didn't know. One of her unforgettable sermons was on dogs. She loved dogs, had studied many breeds, and found them to have similar characteristics to human beings, with recognizable personality traits. All of that was news back then, and the church loved it.

Sister Ursery was fascinating as she shared her vast knowledge and quoted pages of her lovely prose and poetry by memory. She kept everyone spellbound with the many subjects that she spoke on. At one point Sister Ursery had gone to live in California with a shepherd and his family who had huge sheep herds. She slept in tents for days, ate their food and learned everything she could about the sheep and the shepherd. The things that she found out were phenomenal, and she passed them along to her audiences.

One thing the church found amusing was what she told about the young sheep. In order to get the flock into the pen in the evenings, they had them jump a bar. The shepherd knew how high to set the bar for each age group. The young sheep needed a challenge, and he would set the bar high for them. If it was too low, they would just stand there and wouldn't come into the pen. Sister Ursery brought the message home when she likened them to teenagers and their need for a challenge. She also told about the sheep that got injured - how the shepherd would bind them up and keep them close to him. No matter how prone to stray or self-willed a sheep had been before the accident, after being close to the shepherd as he healed, he never wandered again. She likened all these things to the Good Shepherd and his flock.

When Sister Ursery started coming to Brother Hemphill's church it was in the early 50's and Joel was just a boy. But she was already a veteran of the ministry and had preached in some of the largest "Full Gospel" churches in the country. Joel recalls with embarrassment a time when she came to their house on the way to another engagement. Mom and Dad Hemphill were expecting her and had made provisions for her to spend the night with them. However, she came later than they had anticipated, so everyone was asleep when she arrived. It was a sultry Louisiana night and Joel, along with several of the children, had taken their pillows and blankets and made pallets on the living room floor in front of the big fan. Their door was never locked, so when Sister Ursery walked in after midnight and found pallets strewn on the floor, she assumed that they had a house full of company. She shook Joel and he sat up and talked to her. She asked if they had guests and he said "Yes." Then she asked him if they had room for her and he said "No." The poor lady drove back to town and rented a motel room for the remainder of the night.

When Joel came home from school the next day, Sister Ursery was there. His parents were puzzled. They asked him, "Son, why would you tell Sister Ursery such a thing?" But he was just as puzzled as they were. He didn't remember anything about it. He'd been talking in his sleep!

Can Anything Good Come Out Of Bawcomville?

The many times Sister Ursery preached at Bawcomville, she never spoke much about her private life, but it was evident that she had had her share of heartache. There must have been broken relationships, and her desire to bear children was never fulfilled. She had painful memories like most all of us, but she took her pain and brokeness and learned from it, then passed her knowledge to others.

The Serenity Prayer
When Imon Ursery told Joel's family, over half a century ago, that she was the author of the *Serenity Prayer,* they had no reason to doubt it. She certainly had that kind of insight and talent. The prayer says:

> "**God**, grant me the **Serenity** to accept the things I cannot change, **courage** to change the things I can, and the **wisdom** to know the difference."

Her own experiences had taught her that there are many things that we encounter in life that we are *powerless* to change. However, there were things that we can change, and Sister Ursery set out to do that by living for God and preaching the word with all of her heart. At one point she must have realized that she would have to lay some things to rest, put her questions aside, and quit struggling with things that were too big for her.

Though authorship of the *Serenity Prayer*, from time to time, has been claimed by others, it is noteworthy that none of them ever proved ownership. Some fifty years ago Sister Ursery confided to Joel and his family that one insurance company paid her five thousand dollars for the right to use the prayer as their motto. Most of the time "anonymous" is written at the bottom whenever you see the prayer in print, but she never seemed to mind that the world didn't recognize her for the poet she was. The real pay-off is the fact that her words have lived on long after her passing and continue to comfort and speak wisdom to everyone who reads them.

Booth-Clibborn

One of the most renowned evangelists who came to the Bawcomville church in its early days was William Booth-Clibborn. He was the grandson of General William Booth from England, the revivalist who founded the *Salvation Army* in 1865. William Booth's oldest daughter, Catherine, pioneered the *Salvation Army* in France and Switzerland. She married Arthur Clibborn, a highly educated gentleman, who spoke several languages. At General Booth's insistence, the couple combined their names and officially changed it to Booth-Clibborn. Catherine is the subject of the vintage book, *"The Maréchale,"* which tells the story of her life and benevolent work.

William Booth-Clibborn was one of ten children born to Arthur and Catherine. He was a cultured, educated man and an interesting speaker who carried himself with a certain air of dignity, always using proper grammar. He was also an accomplished musician. He played the violin and composed many songs such as *"Down From His Glory,"* and *"He's Coming Soon,"* and was also the author of several books.

William Booth-Clibborn had a pedigree, and it was obvious that he wore it with pride. He only came to Bawcomville out of love and respect for Brother Hemphill, since their friendship began when they were young men through their association with the Salvation Army. Being the off-spring of the noted William

Can Anything Good Come Out Of Bawcomville?

Booth, Booth-Clibborn was in demand as a speaker at big *Salvation Army* events in various countries.

Dad's church was in awe of Brother Booth-Clibborn, but it was easy to see that Bawcomville was a little beneath what he was use to. When he came, Joel's mother became a nervous wreck. She would began cleaning the house days before his arrival because she knew that he would look askance at anything less than spotless.

Several years later when her grandson Joey was a small boy, he went to visit his grandparents and found Grandma Hemphill in a stew concerning her house. Then he found out why. Brother Booth-Clibborn was scheduled to preach a revival at the church, and he was on his way. The morning after his arrival, Joey walked into the kitchen and to his surprise found Brother Booth-Clibborn, who was a tall man, wiping his fingers across the top of his grandmother's refrigerator like an army sargent. He was looking for traces of dust, which there was no shortage of in Bawcomville! As young as Joey was, he then understood his grandmother's apprehension.

Even though he was a portly man himself, Brother Booth-Clibborn came to the Hemphill house wanting to put everyone else on a diet. If he happened to catch one of the children eating sweets such as ice-cream or cake, he'd call them "little sinnahs." Taking all of this into account, its not surprising that his occasional visits were met by Mom Hemphill and the children with a certain amount of dread.

Brother Booth-Clibborn's sermons were very interesting. He had impressive stories from faraway places where he had

The Church

traveled, including foreign countries. One unforgettable story that he told a couple of times was about something that had happened at a large facility where homeless men were fed. The story went that after the evening meal, a man was washing dishes in a large tub that had been placed on the end leaf of a table. The leaf collapsed mid-way of the task and sent the tub full of dishes crashing to the floor. As it fell, the man, who happened to be a Christian, shouted, "Praise the Lord!," and not one dish was broken. This caused wonderment among the men. Could it be that because the man praised the Lord when the tub fell, the dishes were spared?

One fellow who wasn't a Christian hooted at the idea that what the man said had anything to do with the outcome. However, the next day when the unbeliever was washing dishes, the same leaf gave way on the same table with another tub full of dishes. The man let out his normal response, which was a stream of profanity, and the dishes were broken and scattered over the floor.

It was a good story, with a lesson on choosing your words. The only problem was that when Brother Booth-Clibborn told this story from behind the pulpit, he repeated the man's curses loudly, word for word. When he did, he was oblivious to the fact that it sent a chill through the audience and left them stunned. Brother Hemphill was very careful with his words and taught his people to be also. They were told to not even be heard saying slang words such as "gosh" or "heck." But out of respect for a fellow minister and dear friend, Dad let the incident pass.

Sometime later Joel's mother informed him that Brother Booth-Clibborn was coming back for a short revival. With a glimmer of mischief in his eye Joel said, "Mama, I sure hope he doesn't cuss this time." Mom chided Joel and came back with, "Aw Son, he won't do that."

Brother Booth-Clibborn was only there for four services: Friday, Saturday, Sunday morning and Sunday night. Everything went great Friday and Saturday nights. But sure enough, on Sunday morning, with a church full of people, here came the story about the tub full of dishes... (It's not hard to guess the rest)! When he repeated the man's profane exclamation, anyone who looked at Brother Hemphill could see the pallor of his face as all the blood drained from it, and then watch it slowly turn crimson. This time Dad wasn't going to overlook this indiscretion. He was so grieved that on the way back to Brother Booth-Clibborn's apartment after Sunday lunch, he broached the subject. They were alone in the car when Dad gravely said, "Brother, I'm not sure that you should speak in the service tonight." Brother Booth-Clibborn was shocked, and asked why? Dad said, "Our people were wounded by what you said this morning and I was too." Brother Booth-Clibborn was totally in the dark and couldn't imagine what he was talking about. When Dad explained it to him, he was embarrassed and very apologetic, and asked for the opportunity to return that night and make things right. He said, "Brother Hemphill, why hasn't someone pointed this out to me before now? I have told that story for years at large conventions and conferences in different countries of the world! I never realized the impression that I was leaving or that I had damaged anyone."

Perhaps if Brother Booth-Clibborn had ever pastored, he would have better understood the pain and embarrassment associated with the words that he spoke from the pulpit that day. From the beginning of Dad's pastorate, he had gone to war on profanity, teaching his church not to even repeat it. He preached that to do so was "second-hand cursing, and was just as bad, if not worse than using second-hand chewing tobacco!" He pointed them to these words from Paul:

> *"Let no corrupt communication proceed out of your mouth, but that which is good to the use of edifying, that it may minister grace unto the hearers. And grieve not the holy Spirit of God..." (Ephesians 4:29-30).*

Dad and Brother Booth-Clibborn remained good friends for the rest of their lives.

Chapter Fourteen

Poor Little Robin

Poor Little Robin

*R*obert Swinton was a traveling minister from Missouri, and was without a doubt the most colorful evangelist that the church at Bawcomville had ever seen. He was a gifted songwriter, musician, and artist who brought his messages to life with drama. Brother Swinton's parents had been in Vaudeville, and he was a child of the stage. When Robert, also known as *Robin*, got saved and was called into the ministry, he brought flash and flare to the pulpit with him. He wore colorful tailored suits and even painted his shoes to match, with a special water color paint, something he had learned in show business. When he came to preach for Brother Hemphill, great numbers attended to be blessed and entertained by his illustrated sermons.

During his revival meetings Brother Swinton would recruit several young people to go to the church with him during the day to paint props and prepare for his upcoming messages. One of his most dramatic sermons was "The Two Houses," and he used a cast of players to carry it out. He took his message from Jesus' parable in Matthew chapter seven. He said: *"Therefore, whosoever heareth these sayings of mine, and doeth them, I will liken him unto a **wise man**, who built his house upon a rock...**and it fell not because** it was founded upon a rock. And everyone that heareth these sayings of mine, and doeth them not, shall be likened unto **a foolish man, who built this house upon the sand**...and the rain descended and the floods came, and the winds blew and beat upon the house, **and it fell; and great was the fall of it**"* (Matt. 7:21-27).

Brother Swinton started his message with the house that was built *upon the rock.* He illustrated it with a miniature replica of a house sitting firmly on a large family Bible. It was in plain view so that all could see as he delivered his message with eloquence. But it was the second house, the one *"built upon the sand"* that everyone remembers.

Joel and several boys had helped prepare for the production and were included in the drama. They had assisted Brother Robert in constructing the facade of a big house, fastened onto a large step ladder that stood on the platform near the banister. It was an impressive structure made of poster board on planks, and a painting on the poster board of a brick house with a chimney, doors and windows, so tall that it nearly reached the ceiling. It completely hid the stepladder prop that held it, and sat facing the audience.

Throughout Brother Robert's forceful message that night, Joel was unseen on the platform, seated behind the house and hidden by the upright piano. Hardly anyone knew that he was at church. He waited patiently for his cue while guarding a large bucket full of rocks and broken glass. Edwin Howard was situated at the back of the sanctuary near the light switches, also waiting his cue. The sermon intensified when he came to the part where the storm blew and the lightning flashed. Then Brother Swinton quickly went to the piano and pounded on the bass notes to make thundering sounds, while bringing his message to a forceful climax. That was Edwin Earl's signal to begin to flicker the auditorium lights. As the lights continued to flash off and on, Joel poured the rocks and broken glass into an empty #3 washtub. Then he pushed the poster board "house" over the banister. Ladder, boards, and all came crashing to the floor at the people's feet. It was a startling moment! An explosion of sights and sounds erupted, and the sudden outburst caused hearts to nearly fail. Bawcomville had never seen, nor experienced anything so dramatic and wonderful! Sinners ran to the altar to repent, and even people who were already saved felt the need to get saved all over again!

During most revivals, after two services on Sunday, the people were tired so the Monday night crowds were usually sparse, but Robert Swinton wouldn't have that. He started promoting his Monday night service right away, advertising what he was going to preach on, days in advance. For one of those memorable Monday nights, he let it be known that he was going to write a new song within ten minutes and teach the church how to do the same. Everyone's interest was aroused. No one was going to miss an opportunity like that, and the people came pouring in.

He began that night with audience participation. He had those with an idea for a song title, raise their hands. He chose three titles, then said, "I don't know which of these titles I'll use, but I'll be back in ten minutes with a new song." He then turned the service over to Brother Hemphill and stepped into a side room adjacent to the platform to create as the audience waited.

Amazingly he was as good as his word. Ten minutes later he emerged from the room holding a piece of paper with words on it. Then he went over and sat down at the piano and said, "Please be patient with me because, like you, this is the first time I've ever heard this song." Everyone listened intently as Brother Robert began to deliver his new composition. Joel doesn't remember much about the song except that he was impressed at how easily it flowed in poetic rhyme and rhythm. It was definitely a work of art and proved to him that this evangelist was indeed unique.

It was obvious that Brother Swinton was a man of many gifts and talents with a love and appreciation for beauty. But Joel got the feeling that he was at his best during this revival because he had his eye on his sister, Juanita. She was a tall, slender brunette, a dark-eyed beauty who played the piano and sang specials at church. The young bachelors were standing in line to win her affections and her hand in matrimony. Robin Swinton understood that he had a formidable task; therefore he was using all of his creative abilities, but still wasn't making much headway. However, the Bawcomville church was benefitting from his passionate efforts.

Brother Robert had written some good songs, and he sang his compositions each night. "The Beautiful Rose" was his most remembered song. He sang it all through the revival. Then one night he took the title for his text and delivered an outstanding illustrated message. To prepare for the sermon, he invited Joel to go with him to the florist over in Monroe to gather his material.

When Joel slid into the front seat of Brother Robert's flashy Packard, it was on leather upholstery. This was something that Joel had never seen before. To say the least, he was impressed. Then at the flower shop he watched as Brother Swinton purchased three roses, a perfect red rose in full bloom, a beautiful white rose and a red rosebud. Back at the church he carefully wrapped the white rose in a white linen cloth and placed it inside the pulpit.

Poor Little Robin

That night he began the message with the little rosebud, which he used as a type of Jesus at his birth. As he went on with the story of the life and ministry of Jesus, with sleight of hand, he replaced the rosebud with the perfect red rose in full bloom. When he got to Pilate's judgment hall and told of Jesus being beaten and his beard plucked out, he started tearing the petals from that lovely rose and crushed it before everyone's eyes. It was something they could hardly bear to watch. He then wrapped the tattered remains in a white napkin and placed it in the tomb, which happened to be the pulpit.

"For three days and three nights hell rejoiced!" he exclaimed. Then with his voice raised and trembling with emotion, he added "but there was a resurrection morning!" When he said that, he reached into the pulpit and retrieved the napkin that held the beautiful white rose. Then he dramatically held the rose high so all could see it, as the napkin fell to the floor. Everyone got the vision! Jesus was alive, perfect in beauty and splendor!!! At that point, the congregation jumped to their feet and began worshiping in one accord. Hands were raised and eyes filled with tears as shouts of praise went up over the building. Once again, the Bawcomville church was blessed beyond measure.

The two-week revival was nearing the end and Brother Robert still wasn't making much progress with Juanita. He felt sure that all he needed was a little more time, so he convinced Dad, even though he was reluctant, to add another week to the revival. By Tuesday night of the third week, the realization finally hit Robin that the lovely Juanita was not interested. It was a devastating blow to his ego. He was crushed and became testy and irritated, and it began to show up in his preaching.

Can Anything Good Come Out Of Bawcomville?

One night, his frustration came through in his sermon, and he lashed out at the congregation, calling them, "Hottentots and pinheads," because they weren't getting into the service as he thought they should. Most of the people had no idea what that meant and ignored the insult, but a few of them did, and it made them furious! At that point, the revival was over in every sense of the word. It was downhill after that. The redeeming factor was Brother Robin's grand finale that was already set in motion.

He had announced days in advance that he was going to preach a sermon on heaven. The preparation was already underway and included a good-sized cast of church members. Everyone who was involved had been practicing. Costumes were being made, and props were created and painted. Brother Swinton threw himself into the production with fury. He was determined that this dramatization would vindicate him by surpassing all others.

Some of the church was aware of what was going on behind the scenes but bore with his frustrations, and Brother Robert, being the pro that he was, saw his revival meeting through to the finish. Arising to the occasion, he gave the closing message his very best shot.

The big night arrived and once again the sanctuary was packed. Excitement was in the air. Everyone was filled with anticipation. Then the lights were lowered and the curtains were opened, and the audience gasped.

The platform was decorated beyond description. Brother Swinton had attached an abundance of crepe paper streamers to the ceiling and they flowed gently to the floor in front of poster board scenes of blue skies and floating clouds. There were lights on the floor reflecting off of costumes made of white fabric, foil, cellophane, and other types of shiny material.

Sister Howard, the wife of one of Dad's most prominent deacons was a stately elderly lady with a mass of silver hair that she wore wound around her head. None of the members had ever seen it down. But there she stood in a white robe with her hair loose and flowing past her waist. She was holding little Brenda, Joel's baby sister who was dressed in a foil pinafore.

There were others, all dressed in white, even youths of different ages, portraying those who have gone on to be with the Lord *(Phil. 1:23)*. If it hadn't been for that outstanding illustrated sermon with all its inspiration and glittering portrayal of the afterlife, that wonderful revival would have ended on a sour note. But instead, everyone who was there will always carry with them that awesome portrayal of heaven and the saints with their eternal rewards. (Remember, Bawcomville had no TV at that time). It was an ingenious masterpiece that still lingers in people's minds today. Long after Robin Swinton's frustrations were forgotten, that tremendous revival with all of its color, drama, excitement and display of creativity still brings joy to the hearts of those who were fortunate enough to have experienced it.

When the revival closed and Brother Robin left town *alone*, one of the most popular songs on secular radio was, *"Poor Little Robin Walking To Missouri, He Can't Afford To Fly."* The irony of that song, at that particular time, wasn't lost on those who were "in the know" at the Jesus Only Apostolic Church of Bawcomville. Robert Swinton was a fine man with good intentions, who like most of us have, for a short time, allowed

Can Anything Good Come Out Of Bawcomville?

his passions to cause him to do and say some unwise things. But the good that was accomplished far outweighed the blunder.

Chapter Fifteen

Christmas in Bawcomville

Christmas In Bawcomville

*T*he scent of hay and newly cut pine boughs permeated the air and blended in with the sweet aroma of fresh fruit. This was the smell of Christmas at the Bawcomville church and it reached every corner of the sanctuary. It also lifted hearts and filled them with joy and expectancy.

It was the night of the Christmas play and everyone had worked hard to make it a special time of celebration. Another year was swiftly coming to an end and had culminated in this grand occasion of gift giving and the re-enactment of the events that occurred at the time of the birth of Jesus our Savior. The children proudly wore costumes made of crepe paper and tinsel and were excitedly standing by in the back rooms. Some of the adults were scurrying around making sure everything on the set would work as it should (someone was always looking for safety pins), while the audience waited.

Sister Audrey Guess was in charge of the youth and had volunteers to help line out the program. They had decorated the platform with bales of hay placed in a semi-circle with the manger in the center. A make-shift shelter, made of poles, with pine boughs on the top and sides, stood over the manger scene. Someone had cleverly created a campfire in front of the manger from a few dry sticks with a flashlight underneath, shining through red crepe paper.

At the beginning of the program, with the curtain still closed, the "tiny tots," which usually included one of Joel's younger siblings, were the first to perform. They came from behind the curtain, one by one, each holding a square cardboard sign in front of them. It took nine little ones to spell C H R I S T M A S. Each card had a big letter on it, and when the first one came and stood in place he/she quoted the line, "C is for the Christ-child that the babe was to be." Then the rest followed suit, or that was the plan. When they did their part it was a touching moment for everyone because they were so cute and would get mixed up on where to stand and what to say, but they were dressed in their finest and proud to be a part of something so big and special. Sometimes the little ones would end their part of the play by singing *"Away In A Manger."* In those moments something wonderful was taking place far beyond what the eye could see. Nuggets of golden memories were being deposited in small vessels, along with warm feelings of belonging and being special. This was the beginning of these youngsters getting a glimpse of the *"pearl of great price"* and that knowledge would stay with them for the rest of their lives.

The Shepherd Boy
Three or four boys, at the approximate age of eight to ten were always chosen to be shepherds. Only one had a line to remember, *"Come, let us go unto Bethlehem and see this thing that is come to pass" (Luke 2:15)*. It was a grand moment when Joel got to say that line.

The shepherds usually dressed in burlap feed sacks with holes cut out for their arms and one hole at the top to pull over their heads. Their turbans were towels pulled back and pinned from behind with a big safety pin, and they carried staffs that the older men had made from sticks. Joel remembers the excitement as well as the commotion in the side rooms while everyone was getting into their costumes. He also recalls what a chore it was for the shepherds to get to the next scene after the angel announced the birth of Jesus. They had to go to a room adjacent to the platform and crawl out the window, and then come in the front door of the church, down the center aisle to arrive at the manger scene at Bethlehem. The curtains would then open to a portrayal of Mary, Joseph and baby Jesus. The baby, most of the time, was a doll. They had tried using a real baby a couple of years but that didn't work too well. The baby would take a crying spell and disrupt the scene.

The shepherd boys looked upon the *"Three Wise Men"* with a certain amount of envy. They were older boys who got to dress in colorful bathrobes. They would search around for the prettiest ones they could find. Their costumes were completed by nice crowns made from poster board and tinsel. When Joel and the other shepherd boys graduated to being wise men, it was the ultimate.

The night of the play brought all of the work and preparations to a culmination and expectations were high. Everyone took their part seriously. Several of the girls and young ladies depicted angels dressed in white with their long flowing hair. Their wings were also made of white poster board and silver tinsel, either glued or penned on with straight pins.

The Franks family, one of the largest in number besides the Joneses, was much in demand at Christmas time. Alsey, Carl Ray, or Raymond usually had a leading part because of their ability to learn their lines. Their sister Urma Jean was the pianist and was in charge of the music. Shirley, another sister, also had the aptitude to memorize and recite long poems. This family was very gifted and each year made their contribution to the success of the occasion.

After the play everyone would stand and sing *Joy To The World* as the men of the church brought in the boxes of apples, oranges and chocolate candy and placed them on the altar. Then Brother Hemphill would have the congregation line up and pass by. First they were handed a brown paper bag, then they would help themselves to a big, red, Washington Delicious apple wrapped in its own colored tissue, also an orange, some peppermint sticks, and a *Milky Way* or *Three Musketeers*. This was Dad's gift to the church. Then what was left was sacked up and distributed at the nursing homes.

Nothing can surpass the feelings of purpose and belonging that those days brought to everyone. The wonder of Christmas filled their hearts with thanksgiving. The re-enactment of the birth of Jesus always brought "great joy" to the church at Bawcomville and it never grew old. It was a reminder that in the city of David a Savior was born who redeemed us to God by his sinless blood. **While the babe was** wrapped in swaddling clothes and **lying in a manger**, a great multitude of heavenly host was *"**praising God** and saying: **Glory to God in the highest**; and on earth peace, good will toward men"* (Luke 2:12-14).

Chapter Sixteen

Old Burr Head

Old Burr Head

He was a big grey donkey like the ones you see in pictures with packs on their backs, with a wide, dark stripe running across his shoulders that gave him a mark of distinction.

Joel and Daniel had hitch-hiked to the sale barn located along Highway 80 on the out-skirts of West Monroe. Going to the cattle auction was an outing that the two brothers enjoyed. That's how they spent many of their Saturdays, and it was great entertainment...especially the day they saw Old Burr Head. When the scrawny "jack" was led into the auction ring, he was gentle and humble. It was plain to see that he had been underfed and neglected. Ike, the auctioneer, stopped the bid at fifteen dollars and pronounced him sold to Jack Bennett, a cattleman and a friend of the Hemphill family. Joel and Dan wanted that donkey! They came home excitedly telling their Dad about the burro that sold for only fifteen dollars, and Dad's interest was aroused. He called Jack Bennett and he agreed to let Dad have the donkey for a total of twenty dollars, and that included delivery!

In a little while, Mr. Bennett came rolling up in his cattle truck with Old Burr Head standing in the back, and all the Hemphill children were beside themselves with excitement. The donkey was obedient and docile as he was led out of the truck, and they immediately began to play with him and smother him with affection. From that day forward, Dad fed him plenty of grain. Old Burr Head had never had it so good. He was the center of attention and was loving every minute of it. The boys and their friends handled him without any resistance. They would lie across his back, slide off his rump, walk under him, and all the while Burr Head seemed to actually be smiling. Gradually his ribs began to disappear. You could almost see him gain weight daily, pound by pound.

In the fall when the rodeo came to West Monroe, Daniel decided to ride Burr Head in the parade that went through the heart of town. He had fun dressing Burr Head for the occasion. He took one of Dad's old hats and cut out holes for the donkey's ears and put it on him. Then he tied a big red bow on his tail. All the kids were excited and proud of their pet. Daniel dressed like a clown in high-topped shoes, bibbed overalls, flannel shirt, a long tie and a funny looking hat.

But Burr Head's attitude had already started to shift. As he gained weight and his ribs started to disappear, so did his tolerance for fun and games. His humility was fading fast and like some folk who win the lottery, Old Burr Head was getting lifted up in pride. When Daniel rode him in the parade that day the donkey's attitude became more apparent, and for the first time, he'd take bucking spells to try to throw Dan. The bystanders just loved it and thought it was part of the show, but some of the cowboys were unhappy because Dan and Burr Head were upsetting their horses. They told Dan, "Get that jack out of here and don't bring him back!" What they didn't know was, that is exactly what he had in mind!

Daniel and Burr Head finally made it back home but he was now seeing his donkey in a different light. It hadn't dawned on Joel yet, so a few days later he decided to ride Old Burr Head down Schanks Lane with his cowboy boots on. This time the jack threw Joel sprawling in the middle of the gravel road. Joel was

Old Burr Head

able to hold onto the rope when he hit the ground, so Burr Head couldn't get away, but Joel was plenty upset with him. Burr Head didn't realize that he was sealing his doom. By donkey standards, he had become independently wealthy and started acting as though he owned the place. He seemed to have the attitude that the Hemphills were fortunate that he let *them* stay around!

Eventually Burr Head got so bad that if anyone tried to ride him, he would start bucking, kicking, and biting. This is the way things were with Burr Head when Jack Smith came riding up on his bicycle needing a little money. His big saying was, "Hey Joe, I like a quarter having fifty cents."

Jack drew a welfare check from the state, but he couldn't be trusted to handle money. He didn't know how to spend it wisely, so his sister was in charge of dispersing his monthly income. She had an agreement with the neighborhood grocer to let Jack have the food he needed or wanted, on credit. The first of each month, when his check came in, she would go and settle his account.

In order to have cash, Jack did all sorts of things, including picking up coke bottles. He became good at knowing the difference between a bottle that had a deposit and one that was worthless. He called those that were worthless "chunk-aways," and he could readily spot them at a distance. The way Jack made spending money that was most frustrating to his sister was to buy things at the grocery store such as flashlights, pocket knives, etc. on his account, then re-sell them much cheaper. It was easy to sell a new flashlight that cost $1.50 for a mere half-dollar.

On this particular day, Jack was flat broke and the boys were in need of entertainment, so it wasn't hard to get him to agree to ride Old Burr Head for ten cents a time. After the first ride, Jack knew exactly what he was in for, but it didn't stop him. Over and over Jack would climb on Old Burr Head's back, and over and over, he would wind up sprawling on the ground. Jack was thrown eleven times that day. It was a grand rodeo for the onlookers. Joel, Raymond, Daniel, Edwin Earl and Freddie had a ball cheering Jack on and seeing just how long he could stay on the donkey's back. When the show was over, everyone was satisfied. Jack had made $1.10 and the boys had had their entertainment.

Old Burr Head finally became so ornery that he was of no use to them anymore, so Dad set out to get rid of him. But no one else wanted him either. Who wanted a donkey that you couldn't ride? Joel finally gave him to a school friend, but when the boy's daddy got home from work he said, "We're not having that donkey around here! Take him back to the Hemphills." Then they found a man with a goat who was willing to trade him for the donkey, and they made an even exchange. A couple of years later, they ran into the man and he told them that he had used Burr Head to sire some fine mules (a mule is the hybrid offspring of a donkey and a horse). The new owner was happy to have him, and the Hemphills were happy that he was gone.

Joel has fond memories of that old jack, which is probably why we have owned donkeys through the years, and still have, today, one named "Jackie Boy."

Chapter Seventeen

Family Road Trips

Family Road Trips

"You chaps be ready because in the morning we're going on a trip." When Dad made that announcement, it caused quite a stir in the Hemphill household. The children went to bed excited that night, anticipating the big day ahead. The plan was to leave early and return late.

Every so often Dad would take the family on such outings. For him and Mom, it was relaxation and a chance to get away, but for his brood it was excitement and adventure. Sometimes these excursions included Pollock, Louisiana, to picnic and swim all day in Sandy Creek, the same one that Dad had played in as a boy. Those were happy occasions and the family enjoyed planning for them. Sometimes they made lots of lemonade and would gather all kinds of goodies to feast on as they splashed and played until they were exhausted.

The Peddle Car
Going to Shreveport to visit their cousins was another favorite trip for the Hemphills. It was only a two-hour drive from Monroe, and one of those occasions is forever etched in Joel's memory.

Uncle Needie (his name was Cornelius) was Dad Hemphill's younger brother. He was a fire chief in Shreveport, and he and Aunt Frankie and their four children lived in town. About once a year, Joel's parents would load up the children and go spend the day with these wonderful people. However, Needie and his family were not church-goers, which seemed strange to Joel because church was a major part of his life.

One of Joel's earliest memories of going and visiting with their extended family in Shreveport was when he was about six. His cousin, Newman, was a year older than he and had a new red peddle car. Joel was awed by the little car. He didn't know there was such a wonderful thing! Besides that, there was a concrete sidewalk in front of their house on which to ride it. The cousins had a lot of fun that day, and Newman let Joel ride all he wanted to. Then to everyone's amazement, when they started to leave, Newman wanted to give the car to him. The adults were shocked and tried to talk Newman out of sending the car home with Joel. But when they pressed him to keep it, he started crying and insisted. Uncle Needie spoke up and said, "I guess he's tired of the neighborhood kids fighting over it and wants Joel to have it." With that Dad reluctantly put the toy into the trunk of the car and took it to Bawcomville. Joel's good fortune was really hard for him to believe. When he got home, he nearly rode the wheels off the car in the yard and on the gravel road in front of the house.

A couple of years went by before the family went back to visit uncle Needie and Aunt Frankie. Joel was eight at the time, and Newman was nine. As everyone greeted each other, Mom Hemphill put her arm around Newman and said, "Son, you remember your cousin Joel don't you?" He said, "Yeah, I remember him. He's the kid that told me the devil would get me if I didn't give him my peddle car!" Mystery solved. By then Joel had forgotten why Newman had given him the car. What he did remember were the good times he had had with it. Now he, along with his parents, were embarrassed about the whole ordeal, and Dad immediately went home and loaded up the well used little car and took it back to Shreveport. The consequences following Joel's actions weren't fun at all, but he sure had memories of good times with that peddle car!

The Fair
Another memorable event happened in Shreveport at the State Fair, when Joel was a small boy and he got lost in the crowd. On that occasion, as they were leaving the parking lot and entering the fair, Dad gave the children specific instructions to pay attention to where the car was parked. He pointed out several landmarks for them to look for if they got separated from him, which he never believed would happen. One landmark was a big tractor-trailer rig close by that stood high above the sea of parked cars.

When his family entered the midway that evening, Joel held his dad's hand with a firm grip. There was a multitude of spectators, and the Hemphills joined in and began to mingle with them. There was so much to see that Joel could hardly take it all in. The place was pulsating with excitement. People were eating big cones of cotton candy, and the mouth-watering smells of hot dogs and candied apples filled the air and teased his appetite. There were brightly colored stuffed animals hanging all around, and daring rides with flashing lights and blaring music had people screaming to the tops of their lungs. Barkers with loud microphones in front of big tents were trying to get everyone to come in and see "the snake with a woman's head" or something just as bizarre.

At one point Joel wanted a closer look and let go of his Dad's hand. When he reached up and took hold of it again, the hand gave an unfamiliar tug. Joel glanced up and was surprised to find that he had taken a stranger by the hand! Startled, he let go and began searching for his folks, but all he could see was unfamiliar faces looking down at him. That's when he panicked and began running. He ran forward making his way through the press of the crowd, then turned and ran back again, but his folks were nowhere to be found. Joel's exciting adventure had just turned into a nightmare!

After several minutes of running back and forth, crying and his heart pounding wildly, Joel stopped and tried to think. What did Dad say to do if we got lost from him? *Go to the car.* Where was the car? Could he find it in all of the confusion? He then began to backtrack and say to himself, *"We came by here. I remember seeing this"*...until he came to the parking lot. When he did, he spied the big tractor-trailer rig and knew then that he could find where Dad had parked. He then zig-zagged through a maze of vehicles until he found their car. He relaxed with a sigh of relief. All he had to do now was get in and wait. He wasn't afraid any more. He knew his dad would come looking for him. Sure enough, it wasn't long before a figure emerged from the shadows, wearing that familiar hat and flashing a smile with that shining gold tooth. Joel's dad had never looked as good as he did at that moment!!

Vicksburg

All of those trips were fascinating and each one, different. However, the children enjoyed going to the Jackson, Mississippi zoo most; it was the ultimate! But it was the final destination of an entire day of adventure. To get to Jackson, Mississippi from Monroe they had to first pass through historic Vicksburg, the scene of one of the greatest battles of the *Civil War*. For the Hemphills, that meant a drive through the military park where the cannons are on display along with all sorts of bronze and marble statues. You could see the famous generals on horseback and bronze markers describing the fierce battles. That part of the trip was always sobering. Mom Hemphill would stand and read aloud the accounts of those bloody clashes and weep over those who had lost their lives there. Her voice would quiver with emotion and, at times, she would choke up and stop because she could read no farther. The younger children didn't like that, especially Rita. It was just too sad for them.

The old Vicksburg courthouse had been turned into a museum and was filled with *Civil War* relics and memorabilia. There were pictures, letters, clothing, tin cups and plates, razors, guns, knives, cannon balls, anything and everything to bring to reality those brave young soldiers who died in battle so long ago. There were letters describing their hopes of the war ending soon and the pain of separation while being surrounded by death and despair. The names of loved ones, mothers, wives, fiancés, and sweethearts were scribbled on bits and pieces of tattered paper.

Joel and his family took it all in, reading and re-reading everything about that terrible "war among brethren." It didn't take many of those trips for them to get the disturbing picture of a siege that was long and bloody. Because Vicksburg sits on a high bluff overlooking the Mississippi River, the Confederates had the advantage over the Union army with their guns and cannons blocking attacks from water or land. Great cannons boomed day and night from gunboats below, throwing thousands of mortar shells into that magnificent old city. The residents of Vicksburg were forced to leave the comfort of their homes and dig caves in the clay banks for refuge. The city soon was surrounded by the federal army, and provisions became scarce. Toward the end, they had to resort to eating mule meat. But with all of their hardships, it was evident that their southern humor stayed intact when someone humorously printed up recipes on how to cook mule stew, roast and soup.

Then on July 4, 1863, Confederate General Pemberton unconditionally surrendered the city and his army of thirty-one thousand, six-hundred men. The defeat of Vicksburg was so grievous to its citizens that it took them eighty-one years to bring themselves to celebrate *Independence Day* (the fourth of July) again. But by Grant's orders, there was no cheering or expressions of triumph at the surrender because these were their own countrymen. The effect of the *Civil War* was to further establish the Union and bring us together. As soon as the surrender took place, the Confederate army was liberally supplied with food. Grant's men even took their own food out of their hand-sacks and shared with the famished prisoners.

The information depicting the siege and defeat of Vicksburg was there in black and white for everyone to read, and Joel drank it in. Though a southerner to the bone, he was very impressed with Grant when he read his correspondence with Pemberton demanding surrender. Grant commended the bravery of the general and his men with these words, *"Men who have shown so much endurance and courage as those now in Vicksburg will always challenge the respect of an adversary, and I can assure you will be treated with all the respect due to prisoners of war."*

This knowledge came to Joel when he was young and impressionable, and the horrors of the *Civil War* made an impact on him. Knowing that Vicksburg was starved into submission, he was confronted with the accounts of human suffering every time they went there. This piece of American history affected him greatly, and at an early age, caused him to have deep feelings regarding suffering humanity. It also helped produce love and admiration for the great emancipator, *Abraham Lincoln*.

The Jackson Zoo
After the trip through Vicksburg, it was customary for Dad to find a grocery store and stock up on picnic supplies before entering the lovely grounds of the Jackson zoo. There, he would look for a big shade tree to park under and spread their lunch on the ground. It was time to eat to the full and relax awhile before spending time with the animals.

The zoo was humongous and had loads of exotic animals such as chimps, elephants, hippos, giraffes, and of course the big cats. The roar of the lions seemed to shake the ground. It was a sound like no other for Joel. He didn't just hear it, he felt it! After that experience it was easy for him to understand why lions have the title, "king of the jungle."

The monkey island with the moat surrounding it and its rock castles, was the most entertaining area, and was the children's favorite spot to hang around. They loved to toss peanuts in the edge of the water close to the island and watch the monkeys wade out to retrieve them. If none were tossed for awhile the monkeys would hold up their hands and beg for another one. Then suddenly, some special monkey signal would set off all kinds of screeching, and they would start chasing one another in and out of the stone castles. Then just as suddenly, it all stopped and they settled down in total silence. The children couldn't get enough of the silly little clowns and laughed at them until their sides hurt. There were many of them, all sizes, including babies with their mothers, and the monkeys seemed to be having as good a time as the spectators. Actually it was a toss-up as to who was entertaining whom. It could easily be said that on each trip, a good time was had by all!

BoBo - The Monkey
When they had those picnics at the zoo, Dad would usually buy a Jackson paper and after they ate, they would stretch out on a blanket and read. All of the Hemphills loved to read the newspaper, and they read it through and through. Mom enjoyed the *"Dorothy Dix"* column which was the *"Dear Abby"* of that day. The family totally consumed the newspaper from the headlines to the want ads.

One day Dad saw that a pet shop in Jackson was advertising squirrel monkeys for sale for thirty-five dollars, and the kids got all excited! Joel spoke up and said he had saved twenty-five dollars that he would give toward the price, and Anna Gayle said she had fifteen dollars saved and she would gladly pitch in her money to help pay for the monkey and shipping. Joel and Ann Gayle would be co-owners. When they got home from that trip, with more encouragement from the children, Dad put in a call and ordered BoBo (that was the name that they had settled on). The anticipation of BoBo's arrival was the hardest part. The children could hardly wait. Then one day, the call finally came from the bus station for the Hemphills to come pick up their shipment. When they went to get him he was terrified. He had been shipped in a wire cage, and he didn't like it at all! He was greatly agitated and making all kinds of jungle sounds to let them know just how unhappy he was. When they arrived home, Dad wore his leather gloves to take him from the cage, but he was so scared that he bit Dad through the gloves. For the next several days, the children didn't know if they would ever get the chance to play with him. Dad made him a little wooden box; they padded it with rags and put it on the roll-top desk in Joel's bedroom. That became his place of security.

Eventually BoBo got used to his surroundings and calmed down enough for them to interact and win his trust. Joel had always heard how monkeys loved bananas and could hardly wait to feed him one. To his dismay, BoBo wasn't interested in bananas at all. What he did like was grapes. There was a wild grape vine in the back yard that ran along the fence. The kids would take him out there and he would climb along the fence and feast on those grapes. He also loved crickets. In the evenings when Dad made his routine trip to the post office, the kids would go and take BoBo with them. There at the street light where the crickets gathered in abundance, he had a feast at the post office cricket smorgasbord!

At the same time the Hemphills had BoBo, the Clampits, another family from the church, got a monkey. Sadly, a short time later the Clampit's monkey, a friendly little fellow, got into the trash pile and found a jar of old mayonnaise. Getting it open, he ate the spoiled food and died. With that knowledge, the Hemphill children kept a closer watch on what BoBo ate.

Having a monkey in the house wasn't all that they had imagined it would be. He was messy and had to be cared for continually. It didn't take long for the novelty to wear off and he soon became a burden, especially to Mom. After a year or so, she finally put her foot down: that monkey had to go!!

They placed the ad in the paper; brought the price down to twenty-five dollars and Joel agreed to take a ten-dollar loss. The first to come see BoBo was a couple who were engaged. The young man was going to buy him for his fiancé. When they pulled into the driveway, all the children were waiting on them with Bobo. The people didn't even have to get out of the car. Anna Gayle handed him through the driver's window, and the young man passed him along to his fiancé. Then BoBo did a no-no. All of the excitement must have upset his stomach because he used the bathroom all over the young lady! This was something that he had never done before, and Gayle couldn't believe her eyes! The lady was a mess! Embarrassed, Joel and Gayle apologized profusely, but to no avail, and it was no surprise when the couple left without the monkey.

One day BoBo came up missing. All night and all day he was nowhere to be found. They called for him and searched everywhere. The next day Dad bought a watermelon and that afternoon, the family gathered in the front yard under the chinaberry tree to enjoy it. As they were enjoying the juicy melon BoBo slowly emerged from the leafy boughs of the tree with out-stretched hands, begging for his share (which he was gladly given).

Late one evening, another fine couple answered the ad in the paper and came with their two little girls to see about buying BoBo. It didn't take long for the adults to size things up and understand what having a pet monkey entailed. They soon bowed out graciously and said their goodbyes with the attitude of "thanks but no thanks." About eight p.m., the phone rang and it was a call from the couple. They said they hoped they weren't calling too late, but when they got home and turned on the television, there were monkeys on a show and that's all it took! Their little girls set up a howl and wouldn't be consoled. They wanted that monkey! So when they came after him, everyone was in total agreement about the transfer of BoBo. The little girls were very happy to have him, and the Hemphills were glad to see him go - especially since they knew that he would have a good home.

About six months later, Mom ran across the name and phone number of BoBo's new owners and decided to call and check on him. To everyone's dismay, she was told that the little monkey had passed away. They said that in spite of everything they tried, he wouldn't eat and he didn't last long. Joel and the rest of the family were saddened and felt sure that after leaving them, the little fellow had grieved himself to death.

The Ferris Wheel
On one of those trips to Jackson, they drove past a machine shop on the side of the highway. A man was manufacturing small Ferris wheels and had them on display out front. Everyone's interest was aroused so Dad pulled in their drive for a closer look. It was a four-person, manually operated contraption, and the family was fascinated by it. It looked like a lot of fun to the children and would fit right in with the rest of the playground equipment in their front yard. Dad wanted his kids to have things to play with and be active, so he had already bought them a school-ground sized swing set, a tall metal slide, and a see-saw. He had also set up a metal merry-go-round that they called a *"flying jenny."* These things attracted the children of the neighborhood and became the source of many hours of entertainment.

Dad bought the Ferris wheel that day and returned a few days later with his truck and trailer to get it. The excitement was high when he came home and installed it in the front yard by setting it firmly in concrete. To ride the Ferris wheel properly, you had to have the balance of two or four people opposite each other. When a rider came around and approached the ground, he kicked it with his feet and kept the wheel moving.

One day when Joel and a neighbor boy, J.D. Price, were on the Ferris wheel, Raymond Heard who had grown quite strong, got the bright idea to make it go faster. He began to grab each bar as it came around, and pull down hard. It gave him a thrill to see how fast he could make it go and scare Joel and J.D. He was having a great time as the wheel went faster and faster. Joel and J.D. started yelling at him to stop but that made it even more fun to Raymond. Sensing danger, the rest of the children started screaming for Raymond to stop, to no avail. Raymond kept right on making the Ferris wheel turn much faster than it was made to go. Then Joel's seat locked up and instead of swiveling as it should when he reached the highest point it stayed stationary and sent him lurching, head first, toward the ground. He saw the ground coming toward him and knew that if his head hit, he would be severely injured or killed. With all of his might he forced his body sideways, but in doing so, caused his head to hit the large steel support beam.

At this point Raymond realized what he had done and tried to stop the Ferris wheel, but it was too late. When they finally got it stopped, Joel was dazed and blood was dripping from his forehead. The children were horrified and one of them ran and got Dad. He rushed to the scene and began to weep aloud saying, "I've almost killed my darling boy," blaming himself for buying the Ferris wheel. He grabbed Joel up and rushed him to the hospital. It took four stitches to close the wound on the upper right side of his head. The doctor said that it was a glancing blow, but if Joel had hit the bar in the center with that much of an impact it could possibly have killed him. When they got back home, Dad immediately chained the wheel so it wouldn't turn, until he could disassemble it and, in his words, "get it off the place!"

Joel still bears a knot and scar just inside his hairline as a reminder of that unfortunate event, but bears no ill-will toward his good-hearted, well-intentioned friend who was always ready for a laugh and more fun and games.

In his adult years, ministry and music have taken Joel to many exciting places, even foreign lands. But none of his travels left him with fonder memories than those sweet times of boyhood, with his parents and siblings, on their family road trips.

Chapter Eighteen

Joy Riding With Raymond

Joy Riding With Raymond

"**H**ey Joe, wanna go for a ride?" Raymond was grinning from ear to ear as he sat under the wheel of his family's older, but clean, '46 Ford. He and Alvin Jones could hardly contain their excitement when they pulled into the Hemphill's front yard. It didn't take Joel long to decide to join them. "Sure" was his ready reply as he hopped into the back seat.

The car was well kept and still in good shape, and this wasn't the first time Raymond had slipped around and driven the old Ford without his folks knowing it. It was easy. It was started by pushing a button; you didn't need a key! All Raymond needed was *time*, and today he had plenty of it. His folks would be gone for at least an hour, maybe longer.

Raymond's desire for excitement had grown as he grew. At fourteen, he was itching to venture out and became more daring in his pursuit of thrills. The perfect opportunity presented itself anytime his parents were away from home. Sister Heard drove their new car to pick up her husband, who worked in oil fields near neighboring towns. He rode to work with the crew, but Sister Heard had to take him to and from the drop-off point in West Monroe. She had left that afternoon to bring him home for the day. As soon as she was out of sight, Raymond got in the old Ford and drove down about two blocks to pick up Alvin. When they came after Joel, it was plain to see that both boys were savoring the moment of anticipated adventure. They were eager for their friend to be in on the fun, and why not? There certainly wasn't much going on in Bawcomville to entertain teenage boys, and another joyride with Raymond was just one more adventure - the thrill of the forbidden. The few moments of independence were well worth the risk to Raymond, and Joel and Alvin were glad to be a part of the excitement. The excursion didn't last long, but they had a ball for thirty or forty minutes; then it was time to put the car up before Brother and Sister Heard returned.

The boys went by Joel's house and let him out, then on to Raymond's which was down Schanks Lane within ear shot. To turn into Raymond's driveway you had to cross a "cattle gap," which was a kind of bridge made out of pipes that horses and cattle wouldn't cross. It took the place of a gate. Joel stood out in the road and watched as the two boys went down to Raymond's driveway and turned in. He could see Alvin on the passenger side looking out the window and heard him shouting. Then there was a loud "thud," followed by the sound of metal scraping against metal as the bottom of the car slid on the pipes of the cattle gap before coming to an abrupt stop. Joel took off running, and what he saw when he got there made his heart sink. The right rear wheel had missed the cattle gap completely and was suspended in the air. Raymond and Alvin were standing looking at it despairingly. They couldn't believe their eyes. When Joel finally caught his breath he asked, "What happened?" In frustration Alvin spoke up, "Raymond had me to watch and make sure his back wheel cleared. When I saw that he was gonna miss it, I hollered at him, but he didn't listen. All he said was 'Aw, maybe not,' then he gunned it!"

In stunned silence the three boys stood there looking at each other. The big question was, "What do we do now?!" Then Raymond had an idea and spoke up. "If Mr. Swayze's home maybe he'll give me a pull and get us out before my folks get back." Mr. Swayze was their next door neighbor who was retired from the military. He was a dapper man with a mustache and took pride in his place and his vehicles. When he saw the dilemma the boys were in, he had compassion on them and agreed to help. He knew they were in a jam, and Raymond was very much relieved when Mr. Swayze came over in his Chevrolet pick-up truck, bringing a chain. He backed up to the car and attached the chain with intentions of pulling it back upon the road. Mr. Swayze then instructed Raymond to crank the car, put it in reverse, and then give it a little gas to help move it.

There was a lot of tire spinning and slinging gravel. Sure enough, the car began to move, but Raymond had the motor revved wide open. When the suspended wheel touched solid ground, the car went lurching back, and then bolted into the left side of Mr. Swayze's nice pick-up. The sound of crushed metal and broken glass ended with an eerie silence. Everyone was shocked and speechless - especially Raymond. His fun and games had just turned into a nightmare, and it wasn't over. As they stood there sizing up the damage, Brother and Sister Heard rounded the corner and drove right up to the tragic scene. It was the moment of truth.

Brother Heard, a fine Christian man, saw the mess and knew immediately that Raymond was behind it all. When he got his composure, he assured Mr. Swayze that his truck would be repaired as good as new. Then, with all the self control that he could muster, he looked at Raymond and ordered him to "go home with your mother. I'm going to take this car to the shop and get an estimate. Anyway, I'm so mad, if I come home now, I might kill you!!" Of course, by the time Brother Heard got home, he'd cooled off, and Raymond did live to tell the tale - not only *that one*, but many more!

Chapter Nineteen

The Big Tease

The Big Tease

Joel's fondness for teasing his younger sister began very early. Anna Gayle disliked her milking chore, and he had fun with that. Even after she entered her teens and began to have boys call, Joel would answer the phone and embarrass her by saying, "I think she's out milking the cow." At other times when her boyfriends called, he would get on the other line, and as the boy was talking, Joel would "burp" or pretend to sneeze or cough. Anna Gayle fumed and fussed and would threaten Joel within an inch of his life. "I'm going to tell Daddy!!!" was her familiar threat to Joel, and it could be heard around their house often. Sometimes she would just warn him with "Joel I'm telling!!" Either way, he knew that things were getting serious, and it was time to back off.

One particular day when Anna Gayle sounded that warning to Joel, he knew that he had taken his pranks far enough. She had invited several girls to the house for a sleep-over. She and Ann Foster, her close friend, had spent a lot of time in the kitchen that day, making refreshments and preparing for the guests. In a big gallon jug, they mixed red *Kool-Aid*, pineapple juice and who knows what else and came up with a delicious punch. As the finishing touch, they opened a can of fruit cocktail and emptied it in for garnish, which fell down and landed in the bottom. Then they put the lid on the jug and placed it in the fridge on the back porch to chill. Joel was paying close attention while pretending not to. As soon as they left the kitchen, he went and found another gallon jug just like theirs and made another punch. But he used water and vinegar with red food coloring, then chopped tomatoes, potatoes and onions and dropped that in. When he got through, it looked almost the same as Anna Gayle's. The next course of action was to switch locations with the jugs. He transferred hers to the kitchen fridge and put his in its place on the back porch. Then he waited.

At the appointed time the girls arrived and Gayle greeted them at the front door. Then they all migrated toward the kitchen giggling, laughing and talking. Joel followed from a distance, careful to stay out of sight. There was about to be an *explosion* and he wasn't going to miss it! He could hardly contain his delight when Gayle went to the back porch and came back with the fake punch. As she began to pour, she noticed that it had a peculiar odor. Suspecting that something was wrong, she took a sip and let out a yell that would almost wake the dead! Her reaction jarred Joel. He rushed in to quiet her, but she wouldn't be consoled nor quieted, no matter how hard he tried. She was furious because he had messed up her wonderful punch! She was going to get Daddy, and he would deal with Joel!! Joel started talking fast, trying to calm her down but it was like trying to harness a tornado. She was livid! She stormed out the back door, and just before she could get to Dad, Joel ran to the kitchen fridge and produced a glass of her good punch. He showed her that it was exactly as she had made it! To Joel's relief, she calmed down when she realized that her punch was unharmed. But her reaction was more than he had expected. His plan almost back-fired, and he came as close to facing Dad with his foolishness as he ever wanted to. Joel thrived on the wrath of Anna Gayle, but he didn't want to stir up the wrath and judgment of W.T. Hemphill!

The Big Tease

All this teasing and poking fun was just another way of expressing fondness. Joel and Gayle loved each other dearly and were inseparable - and there still remains a special bond between them today.

The Milking Stool
All of the Hemphill children, including Joel, had to endure the cow lot and take their turn on the milking stool, and each had his or her own way of dealing with it. *Ole Bess* was Joel's biggest aggravation. She wore him out by switching her tail and slapping him in the face each time he tried to milk her. Finally he had an idea. He drove a large nail in the side of the barn and bent it. Then every day, just before he started milking, he would catch her tail and hook it over the nail. It was an invention that he was proud of, and it put a stop to being swatted in the face every time he milked.

Anna Gayle passed her time on the milking stool by listening to Elvis Presley. She placed a small radio in the bedroom window, then cranked it up so that it could be heard at the barn. Then she contentedly milked to the beat of *You Ain't Nothing But A Hound Dog* and *Heartbreak Hotel*.

It was no secret that Anna Gayle loved Elvis. Whenever Mom and Dad left for town she would immediately go to the living room, set the radio dial where he could be heard, then flood the house with his rock-a-billy music.

One day the living room was pulsating with the energetic rhythms of Elvis when Brother Richard Coats entered the front door. Brother Richard, an old preacher from another town close by, was all but a fixture around the Hemphill house. He came in and out as part of the family, and much of the time unannounced. Brother Richard's ways were a little peculiar, even to Pentecostals. To him everything was beautiful and had spiritual significance. Often he would get up in church at the most unexpected times, kind of waltz around for a few seconds, wave his hands in the air praising the Lord, then sit back down. The Hemphills and the Bawcomville church loved and accepted him and endured his oddities with due respect.

When Brother Coats came into the house that day, before Gayle could get to the radio and change the station, she was surprised and amused to find Brother Richard dancing around the room and praising the Lord to the beat of *Blue Suede Shoes*! Confident that nothing but *Gospel music* could be playing in the home of Brother W.T. Hemphill, and oblivious to the words, he was greatly blessed by this lively and energetic song!

Anna Gayle was extremely happy when she graduated from the milking stool. Rita, two years younger than she, was next in line. Rita loved to sing, and passed her milking time by belting out love songs and dreaming of her "knight in shining armor." With a song in her heart, she romanticized about her future. Rita was a hard worker and took her job seriously. Even as a youngster she seemed to grasp the value of a dollar and counted her money to the penny. It amused the family that she even washed dollar bills and coins with soap and water and laid them out to dry.

While still in her teens, her "knight," did come along and she married him. He was a fine Christian young man by the name of James Mayo. Once, when the two of them were on a trip to Mexico, Rita became burdened for the impoverished people there and set out to make a difference. By using her own resources, along with donations from others, she has been responsible for building many churches and homes for the destitute - digging wells and supporting penniless pastors there, not to mention distributing tons of clothes and food by hand! This is the same Rita who sang on the milking stool in a barn in Bawcomville, and is still singing today!

Young David took to the milking stool about the same time as Rita. From then on, the two of them became the official milkers. They were proficient at the job, took turns, and buckled down to the task. Brenda also remembers vividly her stint in the cow lot. Hence, the Hemphill home literally "flowed with milk and honey."

None of Joel's siblings seemed to draw back from responsibility. They good-naturally took their chores in stride. Actually it wouldn't have done much good to do otherwise. Everyone was expected to do his or her part. It was a principle that they understood, instilled in them by hard-working, God-fearing parents. Dad Hemphill had a common saying along that line that still resonates with Joel today. He would say, "Son, the world owes you a living, but you have to work hard to collect it." He always said it good-naturedly, with a twinkle in his eye. At other times when Joel would be helping his dad work around the church, he would stop what he was doing, look at Joel with a smile and say, "Son you'll get paid for this when I do," or "Thanks until you are better paid," meaning of course, in the here-after. Even though Joel knew about payday someday, he also knew that it's not *all* pie-in-the-sky. There are so many benefits that come with serving God and having good honest work ethics. Joel has a creative mind, and has also experienced the satisfaction of working with his hands, the pleasure of building and making things happen. A big part of who he is today is a direct result of the responsibilities that he had as a boy - including the time he spent on the milking stool. He still has that stool today, and it's a reminder of Dad Hemphills words: "The world owes you a living, but you have to work hard to collect it."

Chapter Twenty

West Monroe High

West Monroe High

When Joel entered the ninth grade, he transferred to West Monroe High. It was the opening year of their new facility, and a welcomed change for him, though there were quite a few adjustments that went along with high school. Not only did he become part of an eighteen-hundred-member student body, he went from having only two teachers to six, and had to ride a school bus. But the most unexpected change that year happened at home. Juanita had given her heart to a handsome young evangelist by the name of Edward Kelley, and they were engaged to be married.

One day, not far into his first year of high school, Joel was summoned from class to the principal's office and couldn't help but wonder what he had done. When he got there, the principal told him to be seated and began to ask him some unusual questions. "Is your sister Juanita dating Reverend Kelley?" and, "Are you aware that they are about to be married?" Joel answered "Yes sir" to both questions, wondering what this was about and where it was headed.

The principal continued, "Well, they are making a trip to Jonesboro, Arkansas for her to meet his family, and they would like for you to go along as a chaperone. Would you like to go?" Of course he would! When Joel said "Yes sir" this time he could feel the tension lift from his body, and it began to be replaced with a light-hearted feeling of expectancy.

The principal had checked with his teachers and finding Joel's grades good, they gave him permission to skip class for the next two days. With all minds clear, the principal stood up, walked over and opened a door to an adjacent room. There standing in the doorway was a smiling Edward Kelley. He had come for Joel, and after he gathered his belongings and assignments, they headed for the house for Joel to pack his bag. On the way, Brother Kelley let him know that Dad Hemphill had also given his permission. He said that when he first approached him about it, he sensed Dad's reluctance. Then he said, "He can go if you can get him out of school," not believing that he could. Dad hadn't taken into consideration just how persuasive Edward Kelley could be.

Joel enjoyed the trip and the chance to get better acquainted with his soon-to-be brother-in-law. Eddy Kelley was quick witted and full of stories, puns, and jokes. They laughed, swapped stories and had a great time. Eddy also had many thought-provoking sayings. One of his favorites was, "Be true to your teeth or they will be false to you." This clever little statement lodged in Joel's psyche and has made him very diligent in caring for his teeth to this day. No matter how late the hour or how bone tired he is, its floss or Waterpik, and brush!

Another one of his sayings has to do with our thoughts. He was a firm believer in *"girding up the loins of your mind" (I Peter 1:13)*, *"...and bringing into captivity **every thought** to the obedience of Christ" (II Cor. 10:5)*. Anything contrary to these scriptures is what Eddy Kelley called **"stinking thinking!"**

On that get-acquainted trip, Eddy delighted in sharpening Joel's mind with riddles. One day as they drove beneath a low overpass he said, "Joel, I'm going to test your reasoning ability. If you approached that overpass in a large truck and it was one inch too tall for clearance, what would you do?" Joel studied for a while then replied, "I would let about half the air out of the tires. That should get it through." Eddy really liked that answer, and that made Joel feel good.

During that same trip, it snowed. Eddy was very thoughtful and would go out and start the car to warm it up before they went anywhere. Then he began letting Joel go and do it. Starting and warming that new Mercury was big stuff for a fifteen-year-old.

That trip was the beginning of another kind of journey. In those few days, a mutual admiration developed between the two that grew into a strong bond and spanned a lifetime! When Joel started in the ministry at the age of 19, Brother Kelley became a second father-figure to him. He mentored Joel in careful Bible study, teaching him the importance of good sermon notes, good books, careful pronunciation of religious words, and proper grammar. Brother Kelley always sought to better himself. He was a diligent seeker for truth and shared many biblical treasures with Joel, not always in a teaching manner but also voicing his thoughts in general conversation.

Brother Kelley had strong feelings about many things, especially things pertaining to the Word of God. He felt that for a pastor to be fair with his congregation he should never quit digging in the Bible. He was adamant that the Lord's people should be well fed on *"thus saith the Word of God,"* and you could always count on his sermons being full of Scripture and biblical illustrations.

Joel learned much from both men. From W.T. Hemphill, he learned that a pastor should have a shepherd's heart and carefully minister to his flock with compassion. Edward Kelley taught him to never stop learning, continue to grow in the Word and that a preacher's sermons are no better than his scriptural references, which for most men require good notes.

Chapter Twenty-One

The Louisiana Hayride

The Louisiana Hayride

*I*t was the first night of Sister Peggy's revival and after church, she made a bee-line for Joel who was still on the platform where the musicians sat. She took him to one side, backed him into a corner and said with a twinkle in her eye, "Joel Hemphill, I can tell you what your problem is. It's worldly music." Then she fondly slapped him on the shoulder and continued, "God has His hand on you boy, and you had better listen." It was said in love, but Joel knew that Sister Peggy was very serious. She had no way of knowing that he had put together a country music band. He played flat-top guitar and sang lead, his brother Daniel played the upright bass with Raymond Franks on the electric guitar. The three of them were having fun going around performing at local functions and staying pretty busy.

Ralph Beebe, another young musician who played steel guitar in Joel's dad's church, had been going to Shreveport on Saturday nights to the Louisiana Hayride, a popular Country and Western show about one hundred miles away. It was broadcast on KWKH radio and covered the tri-state area of Arkansas, Louisiana and Texas. Proud of its success, the performers on the Hayride jokingly referred to the *Grand Ole Opry* in Nashville as "the Tennessee branch of the Louisiana Hayride." One reason for this was that some of the artists it produced, such as Johnny Cash, Johnny Horton, Floyd Cramer, Jim Reeves, Jimmy C. Newman, went on to greater success at the Grand Ole Opry. The Hayride also contributed to the success of Elvis Presley, the future king of Rock and Roll, who signed a contract in 1954 to be a regular performer, and it became one of the most important decisions of his career. The weekly radio broadcast, along with a live audience, brought him and his music before a large part of the south. When Anna Gayle heard him on that program, she became a devoted fan and listened to him every Saturday night. Elvis even celebrated his twentieth birthday on the Hayride, and the radio announcer described him as wearing pink crocodile-skin shoes, while the young girls in the audience screamed hysterically.

Anna Gayle was thirteen the night Elvis announced that he would be leaving the Hayride, and she cried. She said through her tears, "I'll never hear him again and I won't ever know what happened to him!"

Joel and several of the boys from the church started going with Ralph and began to have ideas of country music success of their own. Joel's love for music, along with a certain amount of talent, made him feel that he could possibly do what they did. He was gifted with a good memory. If Joel heard a song only a couple of times, he could usually sing it himself, word for word. He also had gained experience by singing regularly on his dad's Sunday morning radio broadcast. However, Sister Peggy saw trouble ahead for Joel and jarred him concerning his plans. It was the moment of truth; the time had come to re-evaluate. What *did* he want out of life? Could he hold onto both worlds? Could he sing country music and please God? It was a struggle for a young man who didn't realize that the Lord had a plan for him. But the struggle didn't last long. He decided that even though he didn't know what the future held, he was sure that for him, it wouldn't include country music!

Joel had no way of knowing at that time that he was being tested. God doesn't say "this is a test" when He allows the tempter to set up enticing billboards advertising a beautiful life if we'll veer off the righteous path, just a little. Often God allows these enticements to try our hearts to see if we will choose Him over everything else. Temptation is usually accompanied with the assumption that, "I can do this and still serve the Lord," and that might be true for a while. As in travel, an exit from the main road onto a service road goes in the same direction for a mile or so, but eventually it makes an exaggerated turn *away* from our desired destination.

It never occurred to Joel that his love for music and his ability to play and sing was a gift from God to become his life's work and ministry. At that point, all he knew was that Uncle Billy Brown had taught him a few chords on the guitar, and that his dad needed him to strum rhythm when he wanted to sing. And he continued to polish his craft.

Chubby Stuart, a local country music disc jockey on KUZN radio, the same station that Dad Hemphill preached on, had started *The Twin City Jamboree,* held at the fairgrounds on Saturday nights. Joel and his band were invited to come and sing on that show, a heady experience for local boys. Everything was going pretty well until Sister Peggy came along and pointed out to him that this was the wrong direction. When that happened, Joel found himself at an intersection. The red light was flashing, and he had to stop and decide which road he would take. He also sensed that Daniel was having serious reservations regarding playing this type of music.

No one wants to be just an *ordinary Joe*, especially with opportunity knocking at the door. But their sensitive consciences toward the Lord wouldn't let them pursue country music any longer. They soon dissolved the band, and Joel settled back into his old familiar routine. It was school, church, and painting houses with Daniel. No more fanfare and no more visions of grandeur.

Though unaware of it, Joel had just passed a test, and a chain of events were about to transpire that would bring him face to face with his destiny. He had said "no" to temptation, and with that, God was about to give him a promotion - one that would bring fulfillment like he could never have imagined!

Sister Peggy continued to hold meetings at the Bawcomville church, even after Joel began his own ministry. Once when he was just getting started as a young evangelist, Dad scheduled her to begin a revival, and since she could stay for only a couple of nights, Joel was to carry on the remaining services. Following Sister Peggy in the pulpit was not an easy task. She was a seasoned dynamo. Joel's approach was entirely different, but following the advice of Eddy Kelley, he always studied and prepared his messages. He was never at a loss for words. However, he was acutely aware of the contrast between her rapid fire delivery and his more deliberate style, but he didn't know that it showed as much until after church the first night. One of the little girls came up to him at the end of the service, and meaning to encourage him, said with a big grin and a lisp, "Brother Joel, you can preach as *fast* as Sister Peggy!"

Chapter Twenty-Two

The Gospel Singers

From Indiana

The Gospel Singers From Indiana

*I*n late 1956, an evangelist from Kentucky came to preach at the Bawcomville church. He had a big smile, a winning way and some fantastic stories. Brother Harold kept everyone entertained recounting life experiences, including his days as a Golden Glove boxer. Occasionally he would allude to his band of singers that didn't come with him on this trip. From time and time he would say, "I might send and get my band to come down and join me." When he said that he would also talk about the preacher named *David,* who worked with his band and called him "a preaching machine!"

Brother Harold preached his way into the hearts of the people, and his meeting at Bawcomville was successful. When it ended, Dad Hemphill recommended him as an interim to the Wayside Church in Winnsboro which was once again without a pastor. They agreed to let him fill their pulpit for a short time until a pastor was found.

Soon after he arrived, the crowds picked up at Wayside, and Brother Harold won a lot of favor with the members. His stories and energetic preaching caused a stir, and excitement was in the air. It wasn't long before the report came back to Brother Hemphill that the church in Winnsboro was growing. This was the same assembly that he and his father, Tilman Beauregard, founded in 1920, and because of this they looked to Dad for leadership, and he felt responsible for their welfare. It was also the church where Joel and his family stayed in 1945 when Bawcomville flooded.

The next report that came from Winnsboro was that Brother Harold had sent for his band. The group that he kept referring to as "his band" was a well known gospel singing family from Evansville, Indiana, who had met Brother Harold only briefly. They were known as The Happy Goodman Family and had teamed up with a seasoned evangelist named David and were holding revivals in different parts of the country. Brother David did the preaching and his wife Sue played the organ. This team of anointed singers and preachers was a dynamic package that was connected to Brother Harold only by a brief acquaintance and had no idea he was claiming them as his band.

Enter LaBreeska

The Happy Goodman Family was made up of Howard Goodman, his wife Vestal, his brother Rusty, and their seventeen year old niece, LaBreeska. That's me. It was early in March of 1957 when our group went to Winnsboro, Louisiana at the invitation of Brother Harold. The Wayside church was excited about our coming, and from the first service, there wasn't enough room in the building for the people. The sanctuary was packed to capacity each night, and revival ensued. Many were getting saved and baptized while others were being encouraged and renewed. Brother Harold was so enthused over the large turnout and the success of the meeting that he drove over to Bawcomville one day to let the Hemphills in on the news, and urged them to come and be in service. While he was there he took Joel aside and said enthusiastically, "You need to come and see the girl singer that's with them, named LaBreeska!" Then he went on to tell him more about me.

On Saturday night, the Hemphill family came to Winnsboro to check things out for themselves. Sure enough, when they got there, the people had gathered, and folk crowded in until there was standing room only. Joel and his dad sat on the platform with the evangelists and singers and Joel wound up seated beside my uncle Howard. The two of them struck up a whispered conversation as Howard began to ask questions and make comments about the service. Joel was surprised at how comfortable it was to talk with him and felt an immediate bond of friendship.

Then we got up to sing, and Joel describes his thoughts as we did.

> *"As LaBreeska approached the podium that night with her family I thought, 'Brother Harold was right about this girl. She would stand out in any crowd.' She had beautiful long hair, a radiant smile, and her overall appearance was different than anyone I'd ever seen. I was more than a little impressed by the way she carried herself, and her clothes were modest while at the same time, flattering. When Uncle Howard introduced her, he said, 'My niece loves the Lord and is a good Christian girl. She makes her own clothes and they are nice, but not too nice to keep her from kneeling at the altar to pray with those who want to be saved'."*

Joel goes on to say:

> *"At the end of the service a good many people came forward to give their hearts to the Lord and sure enough, there was LaBreeska, kneeling beside them, praying for their salvation. This spoke volumes to me. Here was this beautiful young girl who was in a very prominent position as part of a famous singing group, down on the floor on her knees. I glimpsed her heart that night and felt that for her, it wasn't a 'show', she was serious about serving God and winning souls."*

The following week, Brother Hemphill invited the group to come to minister at his church. When we arrived, we found the Bawcomville church just as excited to have us as Wayside had been. Brother Hemphill's people could tell that this was not your average evangelistic group. My family was a seasoned gospel singing group with years of experience. And Brother David, as Brother Harold had described, really was "a preaching machine." It was a winning combination.

Of course, I had no idea of the conversation between Brother Harold and Joel about me; however, he says that he was interested in me from the first and wanted to get better acquainted. But there was an obstacle that I knew nothing about. He was going steady. The girl he was dating was a pastor's daughter who lived about fifty miles south of West Monroe. Every Monday after school, he would go to see her, and although they were not engaged, their friends assumed they would get married after they graduated from high school, which was just a couple of months away.

The revival services continued nightly for almost a week. Often I would catch Joel's gaze, but he was careful to keep his distance. Then on Friday night after church, Anna Gayle went to Joel and asked, "Why don't I invite LaBreeska to go and get ice cream with us?" Thinking it was a great idea, he said "Sure." Anna Gayle had nothing against Joel's girl friend, she just wanted to get better acquainted with me and time was running out. Ever the match-maker, she also had something else in mind for her brother. When Gayle asked me if I would like to go, I was delighted and jumped at the chance to be with some young people my age.

I could tell that Joel was proud of his sporty fifty-one Pontiac with fender skirts and a sun-visor, and it was clean and shiny. When we started to leave, Anna Gayle made sure that I was in the front seat between her and Joel. He had in mind the three of us going to the local drive-in, and was unaware of the fact that his younger siblings, David, Rita and Brenda had crawled into the back seat. We were well on our way to the drive-in when to his surprise, one of them spoke up. I had already noticed that the back seat was full of Hemphill children and was thinking, *"He sure does love his younger brother and sisters."*

I found out later that having them along created a dilemma for Joel. He hadn't counted on buying ice cream for that many and didn't have much money. When the waitress came to the car to take our orders, Joel quickly ordered first and specified a small ice cream. He said it loud enough for all to hear and was glad when everyone followed suit. He said that he began to calculate in his mind what the cost would be and was relieved that he had just enough to cover the bill. Joel, Anna Gayle, and I had a wonderful time that night. We laughed a lot and conversation flowed easily. We thoroughly enjoyed each other's company and our new-found friendships.

The revival was to close the following night, which was Saturday; then it would be back to Indiana for me and my family. Joel says that he couldn't let that happen without one date alone with me. This time *he* asked me out after church and made sure there were no chaperones, not even Anna Gayle, who of course didn't mind. When we got into the car, Joel was pleasantly surprised when I scooted over next to him as I had the night before when there were three in the front seat. He really liked that, but he confesses that it was my perfume that got to him. In Joel's words, *"LaBreeska's perfume was intoxicating, and I was thinking that whoever invented ladies cologne knew what they were doing because it was having the desired effect."* (The perfume that I was wearing was a gentle fragrance called *Apple Blossom*, and I had no idea it was even noticeable!)

When we left the drive-in, Joel took me back to the apartment where we were staying. Fortunately, we arrived before the rest of the group. This gave us a few minutes to sit in the car and conclude our visit. Joel then slipped his arm around me and later said how natural it felt to give me a goodnight kiss. But *wow*, what a kiss! That was the moment when Joel realized that he had never really been in love before.

Soon the group arrived, and we all loaded up and headed north. Joel didn't know when or if we would ever see each other again. Indiana seemed so far away and nothing had been said about a continued courtship. But that night left him reeling with some very important feelings to sort out. The big question was, did he really love the pastor's daughter as he thought he had, and as he had told her on numerous occasions? *"What does a seventeen-year-old know about love that calls for a lifetime commitment?,"* he wondered. All he knew was that the lingering smell of my perfume was still on his coat every time he went to the closet, and what seemed like apple blossoms kept bouncing around in his head!

When he got to Sunday school the next day, Joel found out that he wasn't the only one left with thoughts of apple blossoms. Jack Allen was a fourteen-year-old boy whose family owned the apartment connected to the back of their house where the Goodmans had stayed. Joel says, *"He came up to me that morning, obviously taken with LaBreeska as well, and said wistfully, 'Joel I could still smell her perfume when I walked into that bedroom this morning.'"*

By Monday, Joel had come to the conclusion that he probably *"loved"* his steady girlfriend but was not *"in love"* with her. There was a vast difference, and it was time to back off and take another look at where their relationship was headed. A lot had transpired since he last saw her. This time when he went on his weekly visit, he was honest and up front about his date with me. He said, "Even though I might not see her again, the brief time that we spent together awakened me to the understanding that I'm not ready for a permanent commitment." Describing their parting, Joel said that it brought some sadness, even a few tears. There had been no conflict, and though he really cared for her, he believed that his decision would be final. And it was.

Can Anything Good Come Out Of Bawcomville?

Some of Joel's friends at school knew about him dating the preacher's daughter and would often ask, "How's it going with your girlfriend down south?" They were honestly interested, and expected him to get married as soon as school was out. When Joel told them that he wasn't seeing her anymore they couldn't believe it and pressed him to tell them why. Joel then told them about dating this girl singer from Evansville, Indiana. He said, *"I may never see her again, but the time that I spent with her opened my eyes to the fact that I'm not in love with the girl I am dating, and never have been."*

After the break-up, Joel began to reflect on the events that led up to his actions in that situation. He saw how crucial the timing had been and how God was directing his steps. If the Goodman's had waited six months later to come to his part of the country, he would most likely have been married, and that would have altered the direction of his life forever.

Satisfied that he had made the right decision, Joel settled down to life as usual as a guitar player in his dad's church. He began to concentrate on graduating in May, and continued working with his brother Daniel painting houses, which was a pretty lucrative job for a single boy who was still living at home. Joel loved his mother and did not take her for granted; he was glad when he could share his paycheck with her for room and board. She didn't expect that of him, but received it gladly as a blessing from the Lord.

Chapter Twenty-Three

The Tent Meeting

The Tent Meeting

Sister Mary Townsend called Mom Hemphill about once a week to keep her abreast of the church news at Wayside. This time the news was, "The Goodmans and Brother David are back in Winnsboro! They have set up a big tent at the fairgrounds, and the revival meeting has already started."

Hearing that, as soon as Joel's parents were free, they and the younger children drove down to be in service. It was the last of May, school was out and Joel had graduated. He was working full time painting. The hours were long, so he wasn't able to go to Winnsboro with his family that night. He had also laid romance to rest and was in no mood to pick it up again. Joel didn't feel a need to check and see if I was still a part of the group. As far as he was concerned, the time that we had spent together was a fading memory, a brief moment in the past, and he was willing to leave it there. Joel was going on with his life.

When his family got home that night, Anna Gayle, still the match-maker, said to Joel, "LaBreeska asked about you this evening. She seemed disappointed that you didn't come." Those remarks surprised him and rekindled his interest in seeing me again. We'd had no contact since our last meeting, and as far as he knew, I might be engaged or even married by now. He wouldn't have been surprised either way, but he thought, "If she asked about me, that's a good sign." So the next evening found him headed toward Winnsboro.

When he entered the tent that night, he could tell that I was genuinely glad that he came, and I greeted him warmly. Rusty and the rest of the group were happy to see him as well. Immediately Joel was reminded of how comfortable it was to be around my family. Rusty invited him to come back and stay with him in his hotel room and be in the services for several nights. Joel took him up on it, and when he came back, the three of us had a ball for the next few days getting better acquainted. We rented a boat and fished during most days, and there was lots of laughter as we caught, cleaned, and cooked white perch. Then we enjoyed great services each night.

Our time was crammed with activity. Rusty had found a girlfriend, and after church the four of us would go out for sodas. The tent revival lasted for four weeks and during that time, Joel and I were together a lot. But all good things must come to an end, and the time was approaching when our group would pack up the tent and move to another location. When Joel found out that the revival was closing, he went back home and gave glowing reports about the Winnsboro meeting to his dad, and urged him to get Uncle Howard and David to come to Bawcomville. Possibly some, but not all, of his motives pertained to spiritual matters. By then the spark that was ignited between Joel and me on that first date had been fueled by joyful times spent together.

Sure enough, at Joel's insistence, Brother Hemphill called David with an invitation to bring their tent to Bawcomville. Joel learned later that during that call, Brother David held his hand over the phone and asked Howard, "Do you believe that this is God's will, or Joel's?" Regardless, they said "Yes," and the next order of business was to take down the tent and move it and the equipment to the new location. Joel was happy when his dad told him to go to Winnsboro in the family pick-up and haul the organ. He was even happier when he arrived and found me waiting to ride back with him.

Bounding down the highway, we were lighthearted and carefree with the wind in our faces and Fats Domino on the radio belting out, *It's You I Love*. Everything seemed right as we headed toward Bawcomville that day. More than likely, neither one could have verbalized what had happened, but we were already in love. There was nothing we could do to stop it, and there was no turning back. I had lost my appetite and Joel had lost his heart.

The courtship continued as the revival bought us two more weeks of precious time. But we could not have known how swiftly that time would pass. Plans to close the revival the upcoming weekend and move the tent to West Virginia were already set in motion. Joel knew that if I left this time, I might never come back, and he wasn't sure that his old Pontiac would make it all the way to West Virginia. He thought it over carefully before he made a decision. He was absolutely sure that he had found the one he wanted to spend his life with, and he couldn't take the chance on never seeing me again. On Tuesday night after service, Joel didn't make our routine trip to the drive-in for sodas.

He drove his Pontiac to the top of the Bawcomville ring levee, just beyond the church. Then he took me in his arms, told me how much he loved me, and asked me to marry him. It was supposed to be a romantic moment in a romantic setting, but instead it became a battle with mosquitoes. The levee, a barrier for the back water, was at times an incubator for those relentless tormentors. With no air conditioning, the car windows were down on that humid night in June. It soon became evident that whatever was said and done had to be in a hurry. When Joel declared his undying love for me, and popped the question, I quickly came back with a heartfelt "Yes, when?" He had that figured out too and answered "Friday." In Joel's words he says:

> *"That's when LaBreeska displayed her wonderful sense of humor that I would grow to love and appreciate in decades to come. She looked up at me and said with a twinkle in her eye, 'That paper mill sure smells good!' Ever since the Goodmans had been in Bawcomville, they, especially LaBreeska, had a running joke about how bad the paper mill smelled. Many times when we passed it, she would cover her nose and almost gag. She knew that to take me up on my proposal, the paper mill would be part of the package and she gladly accepted!"*

The next day was Wednesday and the two of us broke the news to our families. Actually it came as no surprise and they took it pretty well. But Joel lacked one month being old enough to get married in the state of Louisiana, even though his dad went to his good friend, Judge Heard, for special permission. It couldn't be done. Louisiana would give girls at seventeen a marriage license, but not boys, unless it was a *have-to* case. Since that wasn't a part of the picture, both families agreed that Friday we would drive over to Greenville, Mississippi, about eighty miles away for the ceremony.

Unexpectedly, on Thursday morning the revival had a devastating blow! Hurricane Audrey swept along the coast of

The Tent Meeting

south Louisiana bringing death and destruction. Over five hundred people lost their lives that day, and the Goodmans and Brother David lost their tent and organ. But Joel and I were mostly oblivious to the things that were going on around us, since we were happily making plans for the future, which seemed bright and promising.

On Friday morning, June 28, 1957, three cars pulled out of the Hemphill drive, headed toward Greenville. Uncle Howard, Vestal, and their children Ricky and Vickie, rode in their big pink and white *Packard*. Then there were the Hemphills, Mom and Dad along with Rita, David and Brenda in their new *Pontiac*, and Rusty, Anna Gayle and I went with Joel in his '51 *Pontiac*.

The ceremony took place around noon in the shade of a large oak tree on the courthouse lawn. Uncle Howard signed the license for me as my guardian and Rusty and Anna Gayle stood beside us as best man and maid of honor. We innocently pledged our troth without doubt or hesitation. Brother Hemphill united us with words that were easily understood, and he started by saying, "I guess you kids know what you're doing." The vows were pure and simple. There were scriptures, and a prayer that "God would keep his hand on this couple and bless their union." Then he pronounced us husband and wife.

When Joel said "I do," he left behind those carefree days of boyhood and gallantly assumed the challenge of an adult. He accepted the responsibilities of marriage with confidence and looked toward the future united with the love of his life.

~~~~~~~~~~~~~~

Joel and I have now celebrated our fifty-fifth wedding anniversary and God *has* kept His hand upon us. So for me, the best thing that has come out of Bawcomville is my husband and soul-mate, *Joel Hemphill*! But that's not all of the good that came from there. Some sixty-eight years ago, God called Pastor W.T. Hemphill and his wife Beatrice to establish a church in that remote area. Since that time, it has produced countless saints and church workers, ministers and minister's wives, evangelists, pastors, missionaries, gospel singers and song-writers; people who have answered the call to go forth and spread the Gospel of Jesus Christ to impact the world for the kingdom of God. So you see, *many* good people and wonderful things ***did*** come out of that small village in Louisiana by the name of *Bawcomville*!

Epilogue

Fact Sheet

on

Joel & LaBreeska Hemphill

- Joel and LaBreeska Hemphill have been married for 55 years and have made their home in Nashville, Tennessee for the past 39 years.

- They have sung Gospel music for over forty years, having signed as artists with Canaan-Word Records in 1966.

- Joel Hemphill has written over 350 gospel songs including such classics as, "He's Still Workin' On Me," "Consider The Lilies," "Master Of The Wind," "Let's Have A Revival," "The Only Real Peace," "I Claim The Blood," "The Sweetest Words He Ever Said" and "I Came On Business For The King."

- They have written and along with their family, recorded seven #1 songs which include *"I Cast My Bread Upon*

The Water," "I'm In This Church," "Good Things," "I'll Soon Be Gone," "It Wasn't Raining When Noah Built The Ark," and "He's Still Workin' On Me," which topped the "Singing News" chart for eight months. Over a twenty-year period, from 1970-1990, they had an average #8 song on the "Singing News" Chart.

- *The Hemphills* are recipients of eight Dove Awards and numerous BMI Awards of Excellence. Joel received a Dove nomination as Songwriter of the Year for ten different years. Joel has been inducted into the Southern Gospel Music Hall of Fame and the Southern Songwriters Hall of Fame. Together they were inducted into the State of Louisiana's Delta Music Hall of Fame in September 2011.

- LaBreeska Hemphill is the author of two inspirational books, **"Partners In Emotion"** and **"My Daddy Played The Guitar,"** which are published by Trumpet Call Books.

- Joel is the author of several books such as **"To God Be The Glory,"** a biblical study of the person of God; **"Is The Holy Spirit A Third Person Of God?,"** a biblical

Epilogue

search for the truth; ***"Should We Pray To God The Father Or Our Savior Jesus,"*** biblical keys to more answered prayers; and his latest book ***"Glory To God In The Highest,"*** Removing The Influence of Socrates, Plato, Philo and Greek Philosophy From Christian Doctrine; which are all published by Trumpet Call Books.

- In the past several years, this couple has taken the gospel in sermon and song to many foreign countries, having toured and performed concerts in England, Ireland, Scotland, South Africa, Germany, Austria, the Czech Republic, Honduras, Newfoundland and throughout North America. In 2002 and 2004 they did concerts in Israel, some sponsored by the Israeli Ministry of Tourism.

- Their television appearances include, The Grand Ole Opry, Crook and Chase, The Ralph Emery Show, The 700 Club, TBN, TCT and Gospel Country. They are regulars on the Gaither Homecoming videos and were invited guests at the White House for a big Gospel singing when President Carter was in office.

www.ingramcontent.com/pod-product-compliance
Lightning Source LLC
LaVergne TN
LVHW021559070426
835507LV00014B/1861